UPDATED EDITION
COIN COLLECTORS PRICE GUIDE

Robert Obojski

Sterling Publishing Co., Inc. New York

ACKNOWLEDGMENTS

In compiling the values of coins for this volume, careful study has been devoted to published authorities, as well as prices quoted in recent dealer advertisements and auction sales.

In particular, the book owes a great deal to the cordial cooperation of Burton Hobson, President and CEO of Sterling, Joseph H. Rose, President of Harmer Rooke Numismatists, Ltd., and Lou Pascale, of MTB Banking Corporation, who assisted in the pricing for this new edition. We also wish to acknowledge the assistance given us by André Girard and Michael Francis of the Royal Canadian Mint at Ottawa, especially in regard to providing photos of new issues. We also shouldn't fail to mention John Woodside, Sterling's Editorial Director, who played a key role in seeing the last couple of editions of *Coin Collector's Price Guide* through the presses. Producing *Coin Collector's Price Guide* has taken a team effort.

The magnificent enlarged photographs which appear on pages 8–16 were made by DeVere Baker of the American Numismatic Society. The coins illustrating the various conditions were selected by the Capitol Coin Company.

If I am permitted to add a personal note, I wish to dedicate this modest volume to my late wife, Danuta Obojski, who acted as a tower of strength during the thirty years of our marriage. Danuta, a career librarian, assisted patrons with genuine enthusiasm at every opportunity and at every turn. She touched thousands of lives for the better during her professional career, and at home no one could have asked for a more devoted wife.   —*Robert Obojski*

CONTENTS

COIN COLLECTOR'S PRICE GUIDE
UPDATED EDITION

The *Coin Collector's Price Guide* covers all United States and Canadian coins, from the historic U.S. Continental issues of 1776 to the 1992 Barcelona Olympics and Columbus 500th anniversary issues and the Canadian 1992 set of 13 coins marking the 125 anniversary of Confederation.

Complete with the latest up-to-the-minute retail value—based on auction records, sales catalogs, market reports, and dealer consultations—this comprehensive guide provides valuations for as many as seven different conditions (from "Good" to "Uncirculated" and "Proof") and pictures every major variety, making identification easy. It also specifies individual dates and mint marks (plus recognized collectors' varieties within these groups) and mintage figures for all issues and every major variety.

A Note About Commemoratives . . .

In recent years both the United States and Canada have greatly accelerated their commemorative coin issuance programs. In the 1980s the U.S. has produced five major commemorative coin sets: a one dollar silver and ten dollars gold in 1983–84 to honor the 1984 Los Angeles Summer Olympics; a fifty cents silver, one dollar silver and five dollars gold in 1986 for the Statue of Liberty Centennial; a one dollar silver and five dollars gold in 1987 for the Constitution Bicentennial; a one dollar silver and five dollars gold in 1988 for the Seoul Olympics and a fifty cents silver, one dollar silver and five dollars gold in 1989 for the Bicentennial of the American Congress. All these 1980s commemoratives have become highly popular with collectors throughout the world.

The United States Mint continued its ambitious commemorative program into the early and mid-1990s, with the coins treating a wide variety of topics, including the "Mount Rushmore Golden Anniversary," the "Korean War Memorial," the "United Nations Service Organization Golden Anniversary," the "Barcelona Summer Olympics," the "World Cup Soccer Tournament" and the 1996 "Atlanta Summer Olympics."

Canada turned out silver and gold sets to commemorate both the 1976 Montreal Summer Olympics and the 1988 Calgary Winter Olympics, and since 1977 has struck $100 gold commemoratives on an annual basis. Since 1969 Canada has also released a commemorative silver dollar annually.

In 1992 Canada came forth with an ambitious set of 13 coins (one a $1 value and the others 25¢ denominations), marking the 125th anniversary of Confederation. One of Canada's most attractive recent commemoratives is the 1994 "Anne of Green Gables" $200 gold coin.

Note: All values listed are in American dollars. Values in Canadian currency are slightly higher.

1

HOW TO
DETERMINE A COIN'S
CONDITION

Have you ever noticed how people react to the condition of coins? They take a childlike pleasure in a bright, clear, shiny, sharply outlined coin. Even if it's only a penny, they find something festive and cheerful about a coin when it's brand-new—just put into circulation.

On the other hand, a worn, faded, tired-looking coin, even if it's worth fifty times the value of a shiny penny, evokes no emotional reaction at all. We part with it readily, whereas disposing of the shiny new penny costs us something of a pang.

Well, the man who feels that slight tinge of regret is really akin to the coin collector, who loves coins for their own sake. The physical state of coins—*their condition*—is tremendously important to the collector. A coin in splendid condition is a desirable coin—a miniature work of art. It is likely to be worth considerably more than its face value. But a worn, faded coin is depressingly close to an anonymous metal disc, totally lacking in distinctive character.

COIN CONDITIONS

During the mid-1970s, the American Numismatic Association completed a standard grading system for coins based on a numerical scale from 1 to 70. The scale was originally devised by Dr. William H. Sheldon, a noted numismatist, for his book *Penny Whimsy* (1958), and it has now been adapted for use with the entire United States and Canadian series, thus providing uniform grading terminology. The Sheldon scale can also be easily utilized for grading most world coin issues.

According to Sheldon, the term "uncirculated," interchangeable with "mint state" (MS), refers to a coin which has never been circulated. A coin as bright as the time it was minted, or with a very light natural toning, can be described as "brilliant uncirculated." A coin which has natural toning can be described as "toned uncirculated." Except in the instance of copper coins, the presence or absence of light toning does not affect an uncirculated coin's grade. Indeed, as Sheldon emphasizes, among silver coins attractive natural toning often results in the coin bringing a premium. Moreover, because uncirculated coins may have slight imperfections, there are several subdivisions in that category within the Sheldon scale.

Here, in generalized terms, are the accepted standards for each condition:

Perfect Uncirculated (MS-70)—In perfect new condition. This is the finest quality available. Such a coin under four-power magnification shows no bag marks, lines, or other evidence of handling or contact with other coins. A brilliant coin can be described as "MS-70 brilliant," or "perfect brilliant uncirculated." An MS-70 brilliant is extremely rare, and many veteran dealers and collectors claim they've never seen one. In Europe, the absolutely perfect coin is usually referred to as FDC (Fleur de Coin).

Choice Uncirculated (MS-65)—This refers to an above-average uncirculated coin which may be brilliant or toned (and described accordingly), and which has very few bag marks. The MS-67 or MS-63 rating indicates a slightly higher or lower grade of preservation. In trying to pinpoint grades more exactly, numismatists now often use MS-67+ and MS-64 designations.

Uncirculated (MS-60)—This is called "typical uncirculated" without any other adjectives. This designation refers to a coin which has a moderate number of bag marks on its surface. Also evident may be a few minor edge nicks and marks, although not of a serious nature. A coin may be either brilliant or toned. A true uncirculated coin has no trace of wear.

Choice About Circulated (AU-55)—Only a small trace of wear is evident on the highest points of the coin. Most of the mint lustre remains.

About Uncirculated (AU-50)—Traces of wear are visible on many of the high points of the design. Only half of the mint lustre is still present.

Choice Extremely Fine (EF-45)—Light overall wear shows on all the highest points. All design details are clear and sharp. Mint lustre remains only in the protected areas of the coin's surface, such as between the star points and in the letter spaces.

Extremely Fine (EF-40)—The design is lightly and evenly worn overall, but all features are quite sharp and well defined. Small traces of lustre may show.

Choice Very Fine (VF-30)—Light even wear is visible on the surface, with wear being more evident on the highest points. All lettering and major features remain sharp.

Very Fine (VF-20)—The design exhibits moderate wear on all high points. All major details are clear.

Fine (F-12)—A moderate to considerably worn coin, but still a collectible specimen. The basic outline still must be very clear. All lettering, including the word "LIBERTY" (on coins with this feature on the shield or headband), is visible, but with some weaknesses.

Very Good (VG-8)—A much worn but not altogether unattractive coin. Specimens in this condition should be free of major gouges or other mutilations, but may be somewhat scratched from use.

Good (G-4)—A heavily worn coin. The major designs are visible but faint in many areas. The date and mint mark must be legible to qualify the coin for this rating.

About Good (AG-3)—A barely minimum-condition coin that is very heavily worn, with portions of the date, lettering and legends worn smooth. The date may be barely readable.

Poor—Coins in poor condition are usually highly undesirable and considered uncollectible. They may be bent, corroded, or completely worn down.

As in the case of coins struck for circulation, proof coins can also be graded according to the Sheldon scale. Utilizing this numbering system, the American Numismatic Association places proofs into four major categories:

Perfect Proof (Proof-70)—A coin with no handling marks, hairlines, or other defects. There must not be a single flaw. The Proof-70 may be brilliant or have natural toning.

Choice Proof (Proof-65)—This refers to a proof coin which may have a few very fine hairlines, generally from friction-type cleaning or drying after rubbing or dipping. To the unaided eye, it appears to be virtually perfect, but five-power magnification reveals some minute lines.

Proof (Proof-60)—This designation refers to a proof with a number of handling marks and hairlines which are visible to the naked eye. The Intermediate Grade, Proof-63, is widely used.

Impaired Proofs—If a proof has been excessively cleaned, has numerous marks, scratches, dents, or other flaws, it is categorized as an "impaired proof." If the coin shows extensive wear, then it is assigned one of the lesser grades: Proof-55, Proof-45, etc. It isn't logical to label a slightly worn proof as AU (about uncirculated) for it was never uncirculated to begin with—thus, the term "impaired proof" is appropriate.

U.S. COINAGE ACT OF 1965

Through the provisions of the U.S. Coinage Act of 1965, the composition of dimes, quarters and half dollars was modified to eliminate or reduce the silver content of these coins. The new "clad" or "sandwich" dimes and quarters are composed of an outer layer of copper-nickel (75 percent copper and 25 percent nickel) bonded to an inner core of pure copper.

The clad half dollar struck from 1965 through 1970 consists of an outer layer of 80 percent silver bonded to an inner core of 21 percent silver, with a total silver content of 40 percent. Due to sharply rising prices, however, all silver was removed from the Kennedy half dollars struck for circulation from 1971 on. They are now copper-nickel clad types— identical in metallic content to the current dimes and quarters. Copper also has risen in value resulting in periodic shortages of one-cent pieces. These coins also are now being struck on different planchets—copper-plated zinc. These coins weigh 19 percent less than the copper cents and the value of the metal is far below the coins' face value.

Slabbed Coins

In recent years an effective system of certifying the grading of coins is by "slabbing" them. Coins are assigned a particular grade—say, MS65—placed in a hard, transparent plastic container and sealed. This process is popularly known as slabbing. A panel indicating the coin's grade, certification number, and grading service is also inserted. As long as the seal remains unbroken, the grades are accepted.

Now look at these coins (in their exact size) side by side and notice the variation.

Proof sets

Proof coins are specially prepared with the finest workmanship and materials that modern technique can devise. They are the choicest of all our coins, as far as condition is concerned. This makes them highly desirable coins, as far as most collectors are concerned.

The subject of coin condition is far from academic. As you will see in

UNCIRCULATED (MS-60)

All the details are sharply outlined:

the shield	the eagle's claws
the eagle's eye	the arrows
the eagle's neck	the leaves
the eagle's feathers	the dots in the border
the lettering on the inscription	the lettering on the ribbon

the dots between "United" and "Quarter" and between
    "America" and "Dollar"

this chapter, condition is one of the crucial factors that determine a coin's value and suitability for investment.

In order to describe in detail just how these generalized terms apply to an actual coin, let's examine greatly enlarged photographs of the reverses of eight Liberty Head ("Barber") Quarters.

EXTREMELY FINE (EF-40)

All the details are still distinct.
Note, however, that there are slight scratches on the shield, and that the feathers are slightly faded toward the sides.
There is no proof coin in these photographs, for the high luster of a proof does not show up well in a photo. In evaluating the various conditions, we shall consider 11 features of the reverse of these coins.

VERY FINE (VF-20)

The eagle's eye and neck are distinct, and so are the arrows, the leaves, the dots and lettering on the inscription.

The shield is fairly distinct, but there are some nicks on it, and there are traces of fading toward the sides.

The feathers are considerably faded toward the sides, and the outside dots are beginning to grow fuzzy.

The claws are still fairly distinct, and so is the lettering on the ribbon, although *unum* is a little faded.

FINE (F-12)

The shield and the eagle's eye are fairly distinct. However, there are some nicks and scratches on the shield and the fading toward the edges is getting more pronounced.

The neck is considerably faded, and the feathers are badly faded toward the sides.

The arrows, the leaves, and the lettering on the inscription are still distinct, and the dots in the inscription can be clearly seen.

The dots in the border have become fuzzier than in the previous condition.

The lettering on the ribbon is faded somewhat and several letters are unreadable.

The claws are no longer as distinct as they were previously.

(Note the "D" mint mark under the eagle.)

VERY GOOD (VG-8)

The eagle's eye, the leaves, the dots and the lettering on the inscription are still distinct.

The lines on the shield are completely gone, and the details on the neck have almost disappeared.

Little of the detail on the feathers is left, and the claws seem to merge with the arrows and leaves.

The arrows have grown fuzzy, and the dots in the border are no longer distinct.

The lettering on the ribbon is badly faded and is becoming more unreadable.

GOOD (G-4)

The shield is completely faded; all detail is gone on the neck.

The leaves, the inscription dots, and the inscription lettering are still distinct.

The eye is rather faint, the feathers are almost completely faded, and the claws are no longer sharply outlined.

The arrows are becoming fuzzy, and the dots in the border are considerably faded.

Most of the lettering on the ribbon is unreadable.

ABOUT GOOD (AG-3)

General comment: badly scratched and blotched.

The leaves are still distinct—the only good feature.

One of the inscription dots is clear, the other faded.

The inscription lettering is decidedly weaker than previously; the ribbon lettering is completely unreadable.

The claws are no longer sharply outlined, and the remaining features are completely rubbed off.

POOR

The leaves are still fairly distinct, but all the other details are completely or almost completely rubbed off.

2

CATALOG OF
UNITED STATES COINS

EARLY AMERICAN COINS

Among the coins which appeared before the first regular Mint issues of 1793, there is a great deal of variation, and considerable confusion or obscurity about their origin or the authority for issuing them.

CONTINENTAL DOLLAR

YEAR		GOOD	FINE
1776	Pewter; "CURENCY"	$1400.00	$2750.00
1776	Silver; "CURRENCY" (very rare)		
1776	Brass; "CURENCY" (rare)		
1776	Pewter; "CURRENCY"	1100.00	2500.00
1776	Pewter; E G FECIT	1100.00	2500.00
1776	Silver; E G FECIT (very rare)		

NOVA CONSTELLATIO COPPERS (CENTS)

1783	Pointed rays; "CONSTELLATIO"	30.00	100.00
1783	Blunt rays; "CONSTELATIO"	27.50	100.00
1785	Blunt rays; "CONSTELATIO"	35.00	115.00
1785	Pointed rays; "CONSTELLATIO"	25.00	85.00

BAR CENT

no date (about 1785)		250.00	500.00

Top left: the Continental Dollar, first issued in 1776. *Top right:* the Bar Cent, supposedly designed from Revolutionary soldiers' buttons, with 13 bars for the 13 states. *Bottom:* Nova Constellatio Cent, with 13 stars for the 13 states.

Most of the coins in this group were issued before the United States Mint began operating. President Washington on April 2, 1792 signed the bill authorizing the establishment of the Mint.

WASHINGTON PIECES

YEAR		GOOD	FINE	UNC.
1783	1 cent: draped bust on obverse; wreath on reverse	$25.00	$40.00	$250.00
1783	1 cent: draped bust on obverse; female figure on reverse	25.00	35.00	200.00
1783	1 cent: military bust on obverse; female figure on reverse	35.00	50.00	275.00
1783	1 cent: military busts on obverse and reverse ("double head cent"); no date	30.00	65.00	300.00
1791	1 cent: large eagle on reverse	65.00	150.00	850.00
1791	1 cent: small eagle on reverse	65.00	150.00	900.00
1791	"Liverpool" halfpenny	300.00	750.00	2500.00
1793	1 halfpenny; ship on reverse	75.00	125.00	500.00
1792	eagle cent, copper (rare)			
1792	eagle cent, silver (very rare)			
1792	eagle cent, gold (outstanding rarity)			
1792	1 cent: "WASHINGTON—PRESIDENT"	2000.00	5500.00	
1792	1 cent: "WASHINGTON—BORN VIRGINIA"	1500.00	2350.00	
1792	half dollar, silver (rare)	2250.00	4500.00	
1792	half dollar, copper	800.00	1750.00	
1792	half dollar: large eagle on reverse (outstanding rarity)			
1795	1 cent: grate reverse	65.00	125.00	275.00
1795	1 cent: no date, LIBERTY AND SECURITY	75.00	150.00	500.00
1795	1 cent: date on reverse (rare)			
1795	halfpenny; lettered edge	25.00	275.00	1000.00

FUGIO CENTS

YEAR		GOOD	FINE	UNC.
1787	1 cent ("STATES UNITED")	50.00	125.00	600.00
1787	1 cent ("UNITED STATES")	75.00	150.00	750.00
1787	1 cent: blunt rays	80.00	175.00	1000.00
1787	1 cent ("UNITED" above, "STATES" below); rare			

There are some other varieties, generally quite rare.

EARLY MINT ISSUES

YEAR		GOOD	FINE
1792	half disme, silver	1300.00	3750.00
1792	half disme, copper (outstanding rarity)		
1792	disme, silver (outstanding rarity)		
1792	disme, copper		
1792	1 cent; silver center (rare)		
1792	1 cent; no silver center (rare)		
1792	BIRCH cent (rare)		
1792	1 cent: without BIRCH (very rare)		

The Fugio Cent uses the device of 13 linked circles to represent the 13 states.

One of the many interesting Washington pieces issued by patriotic Americans as a tribute to an outstanding hero.

STATE COINAGE

Connecticut

		GOOD TO VERY GOOD
1785–88	1 cent: laureate bust; seated figure of Liberty	$65.00

Massachusetts

| 1787–88 | 1 cent: Indian with bow and arrow; eagle | 55.00 |
| 1787–88 | 1/2 cent | 75.00 |

New Jersey

| 1786–88 | 1 cent: horse's head and plow; shield | 50.00 |

New York

| 1787 | 1 cent: laureate bust; seated figure of Liberty | 125.00 |

Vermont

| 1785–86 | 1 cent: hillside and plow; eye | 125.00 |
| 1786–88 | 1 cent: laureate bust; seated figure of Liberty | 100.00 |

U.S. MINT ISSUES

The following tables give a comprehensive listing of all the regular issues of the United States Mint. You will note that the values depend on various types of condition, as described on pages 4–16.

The column on the extreme left of the tables gives the quantity of coins issued in a given year. Sometimes a total figure includes several varieties lumped together. In other cases the Mint reports have broken down the quantities that apply to each variety in a given year.

Wherever it seemed essential, individual varieties issued in the same year have been listed separately and carefully described in order to distinguish them from other varieties issued in the same year.

Note also that mint marks play an important part in determining valuation. In most cases—but not all—the *quantity* issued by each Mint will give you the clue to the *variations in value* between the coins of the different Mints.

Half Cents

HALF CENTS—LIBERTY CAP TYPE

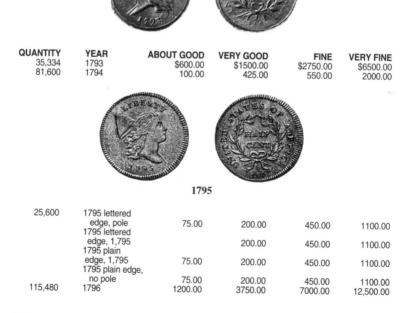

QUANTITY	YEAR	ABOUT GOOD	VERY GOOD	FINE	VERY FINE
35,334	1793	$600.00	$1500.00	$2750.00	$6500.00
81,600	1794	100.00	425.00	550.00	2000.00

1795

QUANTITY	YEAR	ABOUT GOOD	VERY GOOD	FINE	VERY FINE
25,600	1795 lettered edge, pole	75.00	200.00	450.00	1100.00
	1795 lettered edge, 1,795		200.00	450.00	1100.00
	1795 plain edge, 1,795	75.00	200.00	450.00	1100.00
	1795 plain edge, no pole	75.00	200.00	450.00	1100.00
115,480	1796	1200.00	3750.00	7000.00	12,500.00

QUANTITY	YEAR	ABOUT GOOD	VERY GOOD	FINE	VERY FINE
	1797 lettered edge	150.00	500.00	750.00	2750.00
107,048	1797 plain edge	70.00	200.00	350.00	900.00
	1797 1 over 1	70.00	200.00	300.00	900.00

HALF CENTS—DRAPED BUST TYPE

QUANTITY	YEAR	ABOUT GOOD	VERY GOOD	FINE	VERY FINE
211,530	1800	15.00	40.00	60.00	125.00
14,366	1802 over 1800	85.00	250.00	500.00	1300.00
97,900	1803	20.00	30.00	60.00	200.00
1,055,312	1804 plain 4, stems	17.50	30.00	40.00	75.00
	1804 plain 4, no stems	17.50	30.00	40.00	75.00
	1804 crosslet 4, stems	17.50	30.00	40.00	75.00
	1804 crosslet 4, no stems	17.50	30.00	35.00	75.00
	1804 spiked chin	20.00	30.00	40.00	75.00
814,464	1805 small 5, stems	50.00	150.00	400.00	1250.00
	1805 large 5, stems	20.00	30.00	50.00	150.00
	1805 small 5, no stems	20.00	30.00	50.00	150.00
356,000	1806 small 6, stems	30.00	60.00	150.00	300.00
	1806 small 6, no stems	20.00	30.00	50.00	125.00
	1806 large 6, stems	20.00	30.00	40.00	100.00
476,000	1807	20.00	30.00	40.00	125.00
400,000	1808 over 7	40.00	100.00	175.00	600.00
	1808	20.00	30.00	50.00	125.00

HALF CENTS—TURBAN HEAD TYPE

QUANTITY	YEAR	GOOD TO VERY GOOD	FINE	VERY FINE	EXT. FINE	UNC.
1,154,572	1809	$27.50	$45.00	$75.00	$125.00	$500.00
	1809 over 6	27.50	45.00	65.00	110.00	450.00
215,00	1810	32.50	65.00	125.00	250.00	850.00
63,140	1811	110.00	350.00	1000.00	1500.00	3500.00
63,000	1825	35.00	55.00	100.00	175.00	600.00
234,00	1826	27.50	40.00	75.00	165.00	400.00
606,000	1828 12 stars	27.50	50.00	100.00	350.00	750.00
	1828 13 stars	25.00	40.00	80.00	135.00	375.00
487,000	1829	25.00	40.00	65.00	135.00	325.00
154,000	1832	25.00	40.00	65.00	135.00	350.00
120,000	1833	25.00	40.00	65.00	135.00	350.00
141,000	1834	25.00	40.00	65.00	135.00	350.00
398,000	1835	25.00	40.00	65.00	135.00	350.00

HALF CENTS—BRAIDED HAIR TYPE

QUANTITY	YEAR	GOOD TO VERY GOOD	FINE	VERY FINE	EXT. FINE	UNC.
39,864	1849					
	large date	32.50	55.00	85.00	200.00	400.00
39,812	1850	32.50	55.00	85.00	200.00	400.00
147,672	1851	25.00	45.00	65.00	150.00	275.00
129,694	1853	25.00	45.00	65.00	150.00	275.00
55,358	1854	32.50	50.00	70.00	200.00	275.00
56,500	1855	32.50	50.00	70.00	200.00	275.00
40,430	1856	32.50	50.00	70.00	200.00	275.00
35,180	1857	32.50	55.00	85.00	175.00	325.00

Large Cents

LARGE CENTS—CHAIN TYPE

QUANTITY	YEAR	ABOUT GOOD	VERY GOOD	FINE	VERY FINE
112,212 (all varieties)	1793 chain; AMERI	$800.00	$3500.00	$4500.00	$10,000.00
	1793 chain; AMERICA	700.00	2250.00	3750.00	8500.00
	1793 chain; period after date	700.00	2250.00	3750.00	8000.00

LARGE CENTS—WREATH TYPE

112,212	1793 wreath; vines and bars	375.00	1100.00	1650.00	4250.00
	1793 wreath; lettered edge	375.00	1100.00	1650.00	4500.00

LARGE CENTS—LIBERTY CAP TYPE

QUANTITY	YEAR	ABOUT GOOD	VERY GOOD	FINE	VERY FINE
112,212	1793 Liberty Cap	550.00	1300.00	2500.00	6000.00
918,521	1794	50.00	100.00	175.00	650.00
	1795 lettered edge	75.00	150.00	275.00	800.00
82,000	1795 plain edge	50.00	100.00	250.00	550.00
	*1796 Liberty Cap	50.00	150.00	275.00	650.00

*This coin is included in quantity for 1796 cents of draped bust type.

LARGE CENTS—DRAPED BUST TYPE

974,700	1796 draped bust	$50.00	$100.00	$225.00	$750.00
	1796 "LIHERTY" variety	65.00	150.00	325.00	900.00
897,510	1797	30.00	65.00	175.00	325.00
	1797 no stems on wreath	50.00	125.00	275.00	650.00
	1797 crudely milled	35.00	75.00	250.00	450.00
	* 1797 with 1796 reverse	30.00	85.00	225.00	450.00
979,700	1798 over 97	30.00	75.00	225.00	500.00
	1798	20.00	35.00	150.00	300.00
	1798 with 1796 reverse	35.00	75.00	200.00	675.00
904,585	1799 over 98	325.00	1100.00	2750.00	8000.00
	1799	3000.00	1200.00	3000.00	7500.00
2,822,175	1800 over 1798	18.50	32.50	85.00	325.00
1800 over 179	17.50	37.50	75.00	275.00	
1800 perfect date	16.50	32.50	75.00	250.00	
1,362,837	1801	17.50	35.00	85.00	250.00
	** 1801 three-error variety	35.00	85.00	225.00	800.00
	1801 fraction 1/000	20.00	45.00	150.00	375.00
	1801 1/100 over 1/000	25.00	45.00	135.00	425.00
3,435,100	1802	12.50	37.50	80.00	300.00
	1802 no stems on wreath	15.00	32.50	85.00	250.00
	1802 fraction 1/000	15.00	35.00	100.00	350.00
2,471,353					
	*** 1803 small date	10.00	25.00	85.00	250.00
	1803 small date, no stems	17.50	50.00	100.00	275.00
	1803 1/100 over 1/000	20.00	55.00	115.00	325.00
	1803 large date, fraction	35.00	100.00	215.00	500.00
	1803 large date, small fraction	325.00	2000.00	2500.00	7500.00
756,838	1804	250.00	800.00	1250.00	2500.00

LARGE CENTS—DRAPED BUST TYPE (continued)

QUANTITY	YEAR	ABOUT GOOD	VERY GOOD	FINE	VERY FINE
941,116	1805	12.50	30.00	85.00	275.00
348,000	1806	22.50	55.00	135.00	350.00
727,221	1807 over 6	15.00	32.50	85.00	275.00
	1807	12.50	25.00	85.00	250.00
	1807 comet variety	20.00	45.00	135.00	300.00

*1796 reverse has only one leaf at the tip of the right branch. The later reverses show two leaves at the tip of this branch.
**Three-error variety—fraction 1/000, no stem on the right branch and IINITED in legend.
***The small dates have blunt "1"s; the large dates have pointed "1"s.

LARGE CENTS—TURBAN HEAD TYPE

1,109,000	1808 13 stars	$16.50	$50.00	$125.00	$325.00
	1808 12 stars	17.50	60.00	125.00	350.00
222,867	1809	45.00	135.00	275.00	750.00
1,458,500	1810 over 9	17.50	50.00	100.00	375.00
	1810	15.00	50.00	100.00	375.00
218,025	1811 over 10	55.00	85.00	200.00	600.00
	1811	45.00	80.00	175.00	550.00
1,075,500	1812	15.00	40.00	85.00	325.00
418,000	1813	25.00	60.00	135.00	425.00
357,830	1814	20.00	40.00	100.00	350.00

LARGE CENTS—CORONET TYPE

QUANTITY	YEAR	GOOD TO VERY GOOD	FINE	VERY FINE	EXT. FINE	UNC.
2,820,982	1816	$10.00	$20.00	$40.00	$90.00	$400.00
3,948,400	1817 13 stars	9.00	15.00	32.50	85.00	350.00
	1817 15 stars	15.00	30.00	60.00	150.00	1100.00
3,167,000	1818	9.00	15.00	37.50	120.00	315.00
2,671,000	1819 over 18	13.50	30.00	45.00	150.00	550.00
	1819	9.00	16.50	35.00	100.00	400.00
4,407,550	1820 over 19	12.50	22.50	40.00	110.00	425.00
	1820	9.00	15.00	30.00	85.00	375.00
389,000	1821	22.50	55.00	150.00	400.00	2750.00
2,072,339	1822	9.00	16.50	37.50	120.00	800.00
855,730	1823 over 22	35.00	85.00	200.00	650.00	3500.00
	1823 normal date	40.00	135.00	325.00	1000.00	5000.00

QUANTITY	YEAR	GOOD TO VERY GOOD	FINE	VERY FINE	EXT. FINE	UNC.
1,262,000	1824 over 22	20.00	55.00	125.00	450.00	3850.00
	1824	9.00	25.00	55.00	275.00	2000.00
1,461,100	1825	9.00	20.00	50.00	200.00	1000.00
1,517,425	1826 over 25	25.00	50.00	125.00	300.00	1500.00
	1826	10.00	20.00	50.00	125.00	550.00
2,357,732	1827	10.00	15.00	42.50	100.00	425.00
2,260,624	*1828 large date	9.00	13.50	42.50	100.00	500.00
	**1828 small date	15.00	25.00	50.00	155.00	700.00
1,414,500	1829	9.00	15.00	42.50	85.00	475.00
1,711,500	1830 large letters	9.00	15.00	25.00	120.00	375.00
	1830 small letters	25.00	60.00	125.00	325.00	800.00
3,359,260	1831	9.00	17.50	30.00	80.00	400.00
2,362,000	1832	9.00	17.50	30.00	60.00	400.00
2,739,000	1833	9.00	17.50	30.00	60.00	400.00
1,755,100	1834	9.50	18.50	32.50	65.00	400.00
3,878,400	1835 head of 1834	8.50	17.50	32.50	60.00	375.00
	1835 head of 1836	8.50	17.50	32.50	65.00	375.00
2,111,000	1836	8.50	16.50	32.50	60.00	375.00
5,558,300	1837 plain hair cord	8.50	15.00	30.00	60.00	375.00
	1837 beaded hair cord	8.50	15.00	30.00	60.00	375.00
6,370,200	1838	8.50	15.00	27.50	60.00	350.00

*The "8"s of the 1828 large date have rounded centers.
**The "8"s of the 1828 small date have oval centers and a heavy crossbar.

LARGE CENTS—BRAIDED HAIR TYPE

3,128,661	1839 ove 36	$200.00	$600.00	$1100.00	$2750.00	Rare
	1839 type of 38	12.50	25.00	50.00	100.00	375.00
	1839 silly head	16.50	30.00	50.00	100.00	650.00
	1839 booby head	12.50	25.00	50.00	85.00	600.00
	1839 type of 1840	10.00	25.00	45.00	85.00	375.00
2,462,700	1840	8.00	10.00	20.00	60.00	325.00
1,597,367	1841	8.00	10.00	20.00	75.00	325.00
2,383,390	1842	8.00	10.00	20.00	55.00	300.00
2,428,320	1843 type of 1842	8.00	10.00	20.00	60.00	300.00
	1843 obverse of 1842 and reverse of 1844	20.00	40.00	60.00	90.00	400.00
	1843 type of 1844	8.00	12.50	30.00	60.00	375.00
2,397,752	1844	7.50	10.00	15.00	50.00	300.00

LARGE CENTS—BRAIDED HAIR TYPE (continued)

QUANTITY	YEAR	GOOD TO VERY GOOD	FINE	VERY FINE	EXT. FINE	UNC.
3,894,804	1845	7.50	10.00	15.00	45.00	275.00
4,120,000	1846 tall date	7.50	10.00	17.50	50.00	300.00
	1846 small date	7.50	10.00	12.50	50.00	275.00
6,183,669	1847	7.50	10.00	12.50	50.00	275.00
6,415,799	1848	7.50	10.00	12.50	50.00	275.00
4,178,500	1849	7.50	10.00	12.50	50.00	275.00
4,426,844	1850	7.50	10.00	12.50	50.00	300.00
9,889,707	1851	7.50	10.00	12.50	50.00	275.00
5,063,094	1852	7.50	10.00	12.50	50.00	275.00
6,641,131	1853	7.50	10.00	12.50	50.00	275.00
4,236,156	1854	7.50	10.00	12.50	50.00	275.00
1,574,829	1855	7.50	10.00	12.50	50.00	275.00
2,690,463	1856	7.50	10.00	12.50	50.00	275.00
333,456	1857	35.00	50.00	65.00	125.00	425.00

Flying Eagle Cents

In 1857 the Mint discontinued the issue of half cents and large cents because there was little use for them outside large cities, and it was therefore expensive to issue them. The half cents were never resumed, but cents continued to be issued, though in reduced size.

The 1856 Flying Eagle cent is probably the best-known American pattern coin. About 1,000 of these pieces dated 1856 were struck, even though the legislation authorizing the small cent was not enacted until February 21, 1857.

The 1856 issue totalled only about 1,000 pieces. Since they appeared before the 1857 authorizing law, many authorities consider them patterns rather than real issues.

QUANTITY	YEAR	GOOD	VERY GOOD	FINE	VERY FINE	EXT. FINE	UNC.	PROOF
1,000	* 1856 rare	$1750.00	$2500.00	$3250.00	$3850.00	$4500.00	$5000.00	$6250.00

FLYING EAGLE CENTS

QUANTITY	YEAR	GOOD	VERY GOOD	FINE	VERY FINE	EXT. FINE	UNC.	PROOF
17,450,000	1857	10.00	12.50	15.00	30.00	70.00	500.00	3750.00
24,600,000	1858 large letters	10.00	12.50	15.00	30.00	70.00	500.00	3250.00
	1858 small letters	10.00	12.50	15.00	30.00	80.00	500.00	3250.00

*Collectors are cautioned to examine any 1856 Flying Eagle cent very carefully. Altered date 1858's are frequently seen. On a genuine 1856 the center of the "o" in "of" is crude and nearly square. On the 1858 it is rounded. The figure "5" slants to the right on a genuine 1856 and the vertical stroke of the "5" points to the center of the ball just below. On an 1858 this vertical bar points to the left outside the ball. On the altered 1858, the lower half of the "6" is too thick. Some coins are crudely altered and the poor workmanship is obvious, but others are very cleverly done and the alteration can be detected only by careful examination with a magnifying glass.

Indian Head Cents

The Flying Eagle was discontinued in 1859 in favor of the Indian Head design. The first issues from 1859 through part of 1864 were struck on thick, copper-nickel planchets. The later coins were struck on thinner bronze planchets. About 100 pattern Indian Heads dated 1858 of the later-adopted design were made. These were made as specimens of the proposed new coinage and are not actual regularly issued coins. The 1859 Indian Head shows a laurel wreath on the reverse. In 1860 an oak wreath with a small shield was adopted.

1858 Indian Head cent; this was not regularly used until 1859 but about 100 pieces were dated 1858 using the later-adopted design.

QUANTITY	YEAR	PROOF
100	1858	$1750.00

INDIAN HEAD CENTS
(White Copper-Nickel, thick)

QUANTITY	YEAR	GOOD	VERY GOOD	FINE	VERY FINE	EXT. FINE	UNC.	PROOF
36,400,000	1859	$4.50	$6.50	$10.00	$22.50	$55.00	$325.00	$1250.00
20,566,000	1860	3.50	5.00	8.00	12.50	25.00	150.00	1200.00
10,100,000	1861	7.50	12.50	17.50	25.00	35.00	225.00	1100.00
28,075,000	1862	3.25	5.00	6.50	9.00	17.50	125.00	875.00
49,840,000	1863	3.00	4.00	5.50	9.00	16.50	125.00	875.00
13,740,000	1864	5.00	7.50	15.00	20.00	30.00	200.00	1200.00

INDIAN HEAD CENTS
(Bronze)

QUANTITY	YEAR	GOOD	VERY GOOD	FINE	VERY FINE	EXT. FINE	UNC.	PROOF
39,233,714	1864	$2.75	$4.50	$8.00	$16.50	$27.50	$85.00	$1000.00
	1864 L on ribbon							
	rare	12.50	25.00	45.00	65.00	90.00	350.00	12,500.00
35,429,286	1865	2.50	3.50	7.50	15.00	25.00	75.00	600.00
9,826,500	1866	15.00	20.00	30.00	45.00	70.00	175.00	600.00
9,821,000	1867	15.00	20.00	30.00	45.00	70.00	175.00	600.00
10,266,500	1868	15.00	20.00	30.00	45.00	70.00	175.00	600.00
	1869 over 68	70.00	100.00	200.00	300.00	450.00	900.00	
6,420,000	1869	20.00	35.00	60.00	85.00	125.00	350.00	750.00
5,275,000	1870	17.50	30.00	50.00	65.00	90.00	250.00	600.00
3,929,500	1871	22.50	35.00	65.00	80.00	115.00	275.00	700.00
4,042,000	1872	25.00	40.00	70.00	95.00	135.00	350.00	
11,676,500	1873	5.00	8.50	16.50	25.00	50.00	135.00	
14,187,500	1874	5.00	8.50	16.50	25.00	50.00	135.00	700.00
13,528,000	1875	5.00	8.50	16.50	25.00	50.00	120.00	400.00
7,944,000	1876	8.50	12.00	25.00	32.50	50.00	140.00	400.00
852,500	1877	200.00	225.00	300.00	500.00	700.00	1500.00	2800.00
5,799,955	1878	8.00	12.50	30.00	45.00	60.00	135.00	400.00
16,231,200	1879	2.00	3.50	7.50	15.00	20.00	60.00	400.00
38,964,955	1880	1.25	2.00	3.25	5.25	10.00	45.00	350.00
39,211,575	1881	1.25	2.00	3.25	5.25	10.00	45.00	350.00
38,581,100	1882	1.25	2.00	3.25	5.25	10.00	45.00	350.00
45,598,109	1883	1.25	2.00	3.25	5.25	10.00	45.00	350.00
23,261,742	1884	1.75	3.00	6.00	10.00	15.00	55.00	350.00
11,765,384	1885	3.25	6.00	9.00	15.00	25.00	75.00	350.00
17,654,290	1886	2.00	3.00	7.50	9.00	18.50	65.00	350.00
45,226,483	1887	1.00	1.25	2.00	3.50	10.00	45.00	350.00
37,494,414	1888	1.00	1.25	2.00	3.50	10.00	45.00	275.00
48,869,361	1889	1.00	1.25	2.00	3.50	10.00	45.00	275.00
57,182,854	1890	1.00	1.25	2.00	3.50	10.00	45.00	275.00
47,072,350	1891	1.00	1.25	2.00	3.50	10.00	45.00	275.00
37,649,832	1892	1.00	1.25	2.00	3.50	10.00	45.00	275.00
46,642,195	1893	1.00	1.25	2.00	3.50	10.00	45.00	250.00
16,752,132	1894	1.65	5.00	7.00	11.00	16.50	55.00	250.00
38,343,636	1895	.75	1.00	1.50	3.00	8.00	40.00	250.00
39,057,293	1896	.75	1.00	1.50	3.00	8.00	40.00	250.00
50,466,330	1897	.75	1.00	1.50	3.00	8.00	40.00	225.00
49,823,079	1898	.75	1.00	1.50	3.00	8.00	40.00	225.00
53,600,031	1899	.75	1.00	1.50	3.00	8.00	40.00	225.00
66,833,764	1900	.70	.85	1.35	2.50	7.50	40.00	225.00
79,611,143	1901	.70	.85	1.35	2.50	7.50	37.50	225.00
87,376,722	1902	.70	.85	1.35	2.50	7.50	37.50	225.00
85,094,493	1903	.70	.85	1.35	2.50	7.50	37.50	225.00
61,328,015	1904	.70	.85	1.35	2.50	7.50	37.50	225.00
80,719,163	1905	.70	.85	1.35	2.50	7.50	37.50	225.00
96,022,255	1906	.70	.85	1.35	2.50	7.50	37.50	225.00
108,138,618	1907	.70	.85	1.35	2.50	7.50	37.50	225.00
32,327,987	1908	.75	.90	1.50	3.00	7.50	40.00	225.00
1,115,000	1908 S	18.00	20.00	25.00	30.00	45.00	150.00	
14,370,645	1909	1.10	1.50	1.75	3.50	8.00	50.00	225.00
309,000	1909 S	85.00	120.00	125.00	150.00	200.00	400.00	

The "S" mint mark on the 1908 and 1909 issues is at the bottom of the reverse under the wreath.

Lincoln Head Cents

These coins have been issued in bronze since 1909. In 1943 the content was steel, and in 1944–1945 it was copper salvaged from shell cases. All years are quite inexpensive to obtain. The only notable rarity is the 1909 S issue with the initials VDB—standing for Victor D. Brenner, the designer of the coin. This variety was issued in rather a small quantity before the initials were withdrawn.

LINCOLN HEAD CENTS

The mint mark is on the obverse under the date.

QUANTITY	YEAR	GOOD	VERY GOOD	FINE	VERY FINE	EXT. FINE	UNC.
27,995,000	1909 VDB	$2.00	$2.25	$2.75	$3.25	$3.75	$17.50
484,000	1909 S VDB	200.00	275.00	325.00	375.00	450.00	650.00
72,702,618	1909 plain	.40	.45	.65	1.00	2.00	12.50
1,825,000	1909 S plain	30.00	35.00	37.50	50.00	75.00	135.00
146,801,218	1910	.15	.30	.50	.80	1.75	12.50
6,045,000	1910 S	6.00	6.50	7.50	9.00	15.00	65.00
101,177,787	1911	.15	.30	.65	1.25	4.50	15.00
4,026,000	1911 S	10.00	11.00	12.50	16.50	25.00	100.00
12,672,000	1911 D	3.00	3.75	6.00	10.00	20.00	80.00
68,153,060	1912	.20	.40	1.65	3.75	6.00	27.50
4,431,000	1912 S	9.00	10.00	12.50	16.00	25.00	90.00
10,411,000	1912 D	2.75	4.00	5.50	12.50	27.50	90.00
76,532,352	1913	.20	.35	1.25	3.75	6.50	22.50
6,101,000	1913 S	5.50	6.00	7.50	11.00	17.50	85.00
15,804,000	1913 D	1.25	1.75	3.00	6.75	17.50	85.00
75,238,432	1914	.20	.35	2.00	4.00	8.50	50.00
4,137,000	1914 S	7.50	8.50	11.00	15.00	27.50	125.00
1,193,000	1914 D	60.00	75.00	100.00	150.00	400.00	1200.00
29,092,120	1915	.75	1.40	5.00	10.00	22.50	100.00
4,833,000	1915 S	6.00	6.50	7.50	11.00	18.50	80.00
22,050,000	1915 D	.75	1.00	1.25	5.00	9.50	37.50
131,833,677	1916	.15	.20	.35	.75	3.00	12.50
22,510,000	1916 S	.50	.80	1.25	2.50	6.00	45.00
35,956,000	1916 D	.20	.35	1.00	2.75	6.50	37.50
196,429,785	1917	.15	.20	.35	.75	2.00	12.00
32,620,000	1917 S	.20	.40	.65	2.50	5.25	50.00
55,120,000	1917 D	.20	.30	.65	2.75	6.50	50.00
288,104,634	1918	.15	.20	.35	.75	4.00	13.00
34,680,000	1918 S	.20	.30	.50	2.25	4.50	40.00
47,830,000	1918 D	.20	.30	.60	2.25	5.00	40.00
392,021,000	1919	.15	.20	.30	.60	1.75	10.00
139,760,000	1919 S	.20	.30	.40	1.25	2.50	20.00
57,154,000	1919 D	.20	.30	.65	2.75	5.00	30.00
310,165,000	1920	.15	.20	.30	.65	1.75	10.00
46,220,000	1920 S	.15	.20	.50	1.50	4.00	37.50
49,280,000	1920 D	.15	.20	.55	1.50	4.00	42.50
39,157,000	1921	.20	.25	.50	1.00	4.50	35.00
15,274,000	1921 S	.60	.75	1.00	2.50	15.00	125.00
	1922	150.00	175.00	300.00	450.00	1200.00	3750.00
7,160,000	1922 D	6.00	6.50	7.50	9.00	17.50	75.00

LINCOLN HEAD CENTS (continued)

QUANTITY	YEAR	GOOD	VERY GOOD	FINE	VERY FINE	EXT. FINE	UNC.
74,700,000	1923	.15	.20	.35	.70	2.00	10.00
8,700,000	1923 S	1.50	1.75	2.25	4.50	16.00	300.00
75,178,000	1924	.15	.20	.35	.60	3.25	22.50
11,696,000	1924 S	.50	.75	1.25	2.50	6.00	120.00
2,520,000	1924 D	10.00	11.00	15.00	17.50	40.00	275.00
139,949,000	1925	.15	.20	.35	.60	2.50	10.00
26,380,000	1925 S	.15	.25	.40	1.00	4.00	55.00
22,580,000	1925 D	.25	.35	.55	1.10	4.00	50.00
157,088,000	1926	.15	.20	.35	.60	2.50	9.00
4,550,000	1926 S	3.00	3.50	4.00	5.00	12.50	175.00
28,020,000	1926 D	.20	.30	.50	1.00	3.00	40.00
144,440,000	1927	.15	.20	.30	.90	2.50	9.00
14,276,000	1927 S	.30	.40	.75	1.75	4.00	60.00
27,170,000	1927 D	.20	.30	.50	.75	2.00	27.50
134,116,000	1928	.15	.20	.30	.40	3.00	9.00
17,266,000	1928 S	.25	.80	.35	.90	2.75	45.00
31,170,000	1928 D	.20	.25	.30	.60	1.50	22.50
185,262,000	1929	.15	.20	.30	.50	1.25	8.00
50,148,000	1929 S	.15	.20	.30	.50	1.25	10.00
41,730,000	1929 D	.15	.20	.30	.50	1.25	12.50
157,415,000	1930	.10	.15	.20	.35	1.00	8.00
24,286,000	1930 S	.10	.15	.20	.50	1.50	9.00
40,100,000	1930 D	.10	.15	.20	.45	1.00	10.00
19,396,000	1931	.20	.25	.30	.55	1.50	17.50
866,000	1931 S	27.50	32.50	40.00	40.00	35.00	75.00
4,480,000	1931 D	2.75	3.25	3.50	4.00	7.00	55.00
9,962,000	1932	1.00	1.25	1.50	2.00	2.75	18.50
10,500,000	1932 D	.65	.75	1.25	2.00	2.50	16.50
14,360,000	1933	.50	.60	.70	.90	2.50	18.50
6,200,000	1933 D	1.75	2.00	2.25	2.50	4.00	25.00

QUANTITY	YEAR	UNC.	QUANTITY	YEAR	UNC.
219,080,000	1934	$4.00	181,770,000	1945 S copper	.75
28,446,000	1934 D	22.50	226,268,000	1945 D copper	.85
245,388,000	1935	1.75	991,655,000	1946	.35
38,702,000	1935 S	7.50	198,100,000	1946 S	.75
47,000,000	1935 D	3.50	315,690,000	1946 D	.35
309,637,569	1936	2.00	190,555,000	1947	1.00
29,130,000	1936 S	2.00	99,000,000	1947 S	1.00
40,620,000	1936 D	1.75	194,750,000	1947 D	.50
309,179,320	1937	1.75	317,570,000	1948	.75
34,500,000	1937 S	2.00	81,735,000	1948 S	1.25
50,430,000	1937 D	2.00	172,637,500	1948 D	.60
156,696,734	1938	1.85	217,490,000	1949	1.15
15,180,000	1938 S	4.00	64,290,000	1949 S	2.75
20,010,000	1938 D	3.00	154,370,500	1949 D	.85
316,479,520	1939	1.25	272,686,386	1950	.75
52,070,000	1939 S	1.75	118,505,000	1950 S	1.15
15,160,000	1939 D	6.00	334,950,000	1950 D	.50
586,825,872	1940	1.00	294,633,500	1951	2.00
112,940,000	1940 S	.90	100,890,000	1951 S	1.50
81,390,000	1940 D	1.00	625,355,000	1951 D	.50
887,039,100	1941	.75	186,856,980	1952	.85
92,360,000	1941 S	4.00	137,800,004	1952 S	1.25
128,700,000	1941 D	3.00	746,130,000	1952 D	.50
657,828,600	1942	.50	256,883,800	1953	.50
85,590,000	1942 S	5.00	181,835,000	1953 S	.75
206,698,000	1942 D	.70	700,515,000	1953 D	.40
684,628,670	1943 zinc-steel	1.00	96,190,000	1954 S	.50
191,550,000	1943 S zinc-steel	2.00	251,552,500	1954 D	.35
217,660,000	1943 D zinc-steel	1.00	330,958,200	1955	.30
1,435,400,000	1944 copper	.75	44,610,000	1955 S	.60
71,873,350	1954	1.00	563,257,500	1955 D	.25
282,760,000	1944 S copper	.65	420,926,081	1956	.25
430,587,000	1944 D copper	.60	1,098,201,100	1956 D	.25
1,040,515,000	1945 copper	.40	282,540,000	1957	.25

LINCOLN HEAD CENTS (continued)

1955 Double die
VF 350.00 Unc 1500.00

QUANTITY	YEAR	UNC.
4,674,292,426	1976	.10
4,221,592,455	1976 D	.10
4,149,730	1975 S (proof only)	
4,469,930,000	1977	.10
4,194,062,300	1977 D	.10
3,251,152	1977 S (proof only)	
5,558,605,000	1978	.10
4,280,233,400	1978 D	.10
3,127,781	1978 S (proof only)	
6,018,515,000	1979	.10
4,139,357,254	1979 D	.10
3,677,175	1979 S (proof only)	
7,414,705,000	1980	.10
5,140,098,660	1980 D	.10
3,554,806	1980 S (proof only)	
7,491,750,000	1981	.10
5,373,235,677	1981 D	.10
4,063,083	1981 S (proof only)	
10,712,525,000	1982 Large Date	.10
	1982 Small Date	.15
6,012,979,368	1982 D	.10
3,857,479	1982 S (proof only)	
7,752,355,000	1983 Double Die	
	Reverse	200.00
	1983	.10
6,467,198,428	1983 D	.10
3,228,648	1983 S (proof only)	
8,151,079,000	1984	.10
5,569,238,906	1984 D	.10
3,065,110	1984 S (proof only)	
5,648,489,887	1985	.10
5,287,399,926	1985 D	.10
3,362,662	1985 S (proof only)	
4,491,395,493	1986	.10
4,442,866,698	1986 D	.10
3,010,497	1986 S (proof only)	
4,682,246,693	1987	.10
4,879,389,514	1987 D	.10
3,792,233	1987 S (proof only)	
6,092,810,000	1988	.10
5,253,740,443	1988 D	.10
3,262,948	1988 S (proof only)	
7,261,535,000	1989	.10
5,345,467,111	1989 D	.10
3,215,728	1989 S (proof only)	
6,851,765,000	1990	.10
4,922,894,533	1990 D	.10
3,299,559	1990 S (proof only)	
5,165,940,000	1991	.10
4,158,442,076	1991 D	.10
2,867,787	1991 S (proof only)	
4,648,905,000	1992	.10
4,448,673,300	1992 D	.10
4,176,560	1992 S (proof only)	.10
5,684,705,000	1993	.10
6,426,650,571	1993 D	.10
3,394,792	1993 S (proof only)	.10
	1994	.10
	1994 D	.10
	1994 S (proof only)	.10
	1995	.10
	1995 D	.10
	1995 S (proof only)	.10

QUANTITY	YEAR	MS-65
1,051,342,000	1957 D	.25
252,595,000	1958	.25
800,953,300	1958 D	.20
619,715,000	1959	.20
1,279,760,000	1959 D	.20
586,405,000	1960 Small date	6.50
	1960 Large date	.20
1,580,884,000	1960 D Small date	.50
	1960 D Large date	.20
756,373,244	1961	.20
1,753,266,700	1961 D	.20
609,263,019	1962	.20
1,793,148,400	1962 D	.20
757,185,645	1963	.20
1,774,020,400	1963 D	.20
2,648,575,000	1964	.15
3,799,071,500	1964 D	.15
1,494,884,900	1965	.15
2,185,886,200	1966	.15
3,048,667,100	1967	.15
1,707,880,970	1968	.15
2,886,269,600	1968 D	.15
258,270,001	1968 S	.15
1,136,910,000	1969	.15
4,002,832,200	1969 D	.15
544,375,000	1969 S	.15
1,898,315,000	1970	.15
2,891,438,900	1970 D	.15
693,192,814	1970 S	.15
1,919,490,000	1971	.15
2,911,045,600	1971 D	.15
528,354,192	1971 S	.10
	1972 Double strike	275.00
2,933,255,000	1972	.15
2,665,071,400	1972 D	.15
380,200,104	1972 S	.15
3,728,245,000	1973	.15
3,549,576,588	1973 D	.15
319,937,634	1973 S	.15
4,232,140,523	1974	.15
4,235,098,000	1974 D	.15
412,039,228	1974 S	.15
5,451,476,142	1975	
4,505,275,300	1975 D	.10
2,845,450	1975 S (proof only)	

Two Cent Pieces

TWO CENTS—BRONZE

QUANTITY	YEAR	GOOD TO VERY GOOD	VERY FINE	EXT. FINE	FINE	UNC.	PROOF -63
19,847,500	1864 small motto	$55.00	$85.00	$110.00	$200.00	$550.00	
	1864 large motto	6.00	8.00	12.50	30.00	225.00	1000.00
13,640,000	1865	6.00	8.00	12.50	30.00	225.00	900.00
3,177,000	1866	6.00	8.00	12.50	30.00	235.00	900.00
2,938,750	1867	6.00	8.00	12.50	30.00	235.00	900.00
2,803,750	1868	6.00	8.00	12.50	30.00	235.00	900.00
1,546,500	1869	6.00	8.00	12.50	30.00	235.00	900.00
861,250	1870	7.50	15.00	25.00	50.00	300.00	900.00
721,250	1871	8.50	17.50	27.50	60.00	350.00	900.00
65,000	1872	65.00	160.00	165.00	225.00	850.00	1400.00
?	1873 only proofs were struck						2500.00

Three Cent Pieces

THREE CENTS—SILVER

1851–1853   1854–1873

The "O" mint mark is to the right of the "III" on the reverse.

QUANTITY	YEAR	GOOD TO VERY GOOD	VERY FINE	EXT. FINE	FINE	UNC.	PROOF -63
5,447,400	1851	$9.00	$13.00	$25.00	$45.00	$275.00	
720,000	1851 O	12.50	25.00	50.00	75.00	425.00	
18,663,500	1852	9.00	13.00	25.00	45.00	275.00	
11,400,000	1853	9.00	13.00	25.00	45.00	275.00	
671,000	1854	13.00	20.00	30.00	70.00	450.00	
139,000	1855	17.50	27.50	50.00	125.00	550.00	3250.00
1,458,000	1856	13.00	20.00	30.00	60.00	450.00	2500.00
1,042,000	1857	11.00	16.00	30.00	65.00	450.00	2500.00
1,604,000	1858	11.00	16.00	30.00	65.00	500.00	2500.00
365,000	1859	12.50	16.00	25.00	55.00	275.00	800.00
287,000	1860	12.50	16.00	25.00	55.00	275.00	800.00
498,000	1861	12.50	16.00	25.00	55.00	275.00	800.00
363,550	1862	12.50	16.00	25.00	55.00	275.00	900.00
21,460	1863	(all remaining years struck as proofs only)					950.00
470	1864						950.00
8,500	1865						950.00

QUANTITY	YEAR	GOOD TO VERY GOOD	VERY FINE	EXT. FINE	FINE	UNC.	PROOF -63
22,725	1866						900.00
4,625	1867						900.00
4,100	1868						900.00
5,100	1869						900.00
4,000	1870						900.00
4,260	1871						900.00
1,950	1872						900.00
600	1873						1250.00

THREE CENTS—NICKEL

QUANTITY	YEAR	GOOD TO VERY GOOD	VERY FINE	EXT. FINE	FINE	UNC.	PROOF -63
11,382,000	1865	$5.50	$7.00	$9.00	$15.00	$135.00	$1200.00
4,801,000	1866	5.50	7.00	9.00	15.00	135.00	500.00
3,915,000	1867	5.50	7.00	9.00	15.00	150.00	400.00
3,252,000	1868	5.50	7.00	9.00	15.00	150.00	400.00
1,604,000	1869	5.50	8.00	11.00	15.00	150.00	400.00
1,335,000	1870	5.50	8.50	10.00	16.00	150.00	400.00
604,000	1871	6.00	9.00	11.00	17.50	175.00	400.00
862,000	1872	6.00	9.00	11.00	17.50	175.00	400.00
1,173,000	1873	6.00	9.00	11.00	17.50	150.00	400.00
790,000	1874	6.00	9.00	11.00	25.00	175.00	400.00
228,000	1875	7.50	12.50	17.50	25.00	200.00	400.00
162,000	1876	8.00	12.00	17.50		225.00	400.00
?	1877 only proofs were struck						1750.00
2,350	1878 only proofs were struck						900.00
41,200	1879	35.00	40.00	50.00	60.00	275.00	400.00
24,955	1880	40.00	45.00	70.00	80.00	275.00	400.00
1,080,575	1881	6.00	8.00	10.00	15.00	135.00	400.00
25,300	1882	37.50	50.00	60.00	70.00	275.00	400.00
10,609	1883	75.00	100.00	125.00	150.00	300.00	400.00
5,642	1884	100.00	150.00	175.00	200.00	400.00	700.00
4,790	1885	175.00	225.00	250.00	300.00	425.00	800.00
4,290	1886 only proofs were struck						800.00
7,961	1887	150.00	175.00	200.00	225.00	300.00	800.00
	1887 over 86—only proofs were struck						625.00
41,083	1888	35.00	37.50	45.00	50.00	250.00	425.00
21,561	1889	40.00	50.00	55.00	70.00	300.00	425.00

These now obsolete denominations were each introduced to fill a specific need. The two cent piece was an attempt to cope with the desperate shortage of small coins that occurred near the close of the Civil War. The theory was that a coin press could produce just as many two cent pieces as one cent pieces in a given time, but the face value of the coins going into circulation would be double. Once the deficiency was made up, the larger coins proved to be awkward. The silver three cent piece came into being along with the 3¢ letter rate with the thought that it would be convenient for buying stamps. The nickel three cent piece which came later was intended to redeem the three cent paper notes issued during the Civil War. Neither of the three cent coins was really practical and after the first few years they were struck in small quantities only until they were finally discontinued.

Nickel Five Cents

Though nickel was suggested for American coins as early as 1837, the first five-cent nickels were not issued until 1866.

NICKEL FIVE CENTS—SHIELD TYPE

1866–1867   1867–1883

QUANTITY	YEAR	GOOD TO VERY GOOD	FINE	VERY FINE	EXT. FINE	UNC.	PROOF -63
14,742,500	1866	$11.00	$18.50	$32.50	$85.00	$415.00	$2500.00
30,909,500	1867						
	with rays	13.50	25.00	35.00	90.00	425.00	8000.00
	1867 without rays	8.00	12.50	17.50	35.00	150.00	425.00
28,817,000	1868	8.00	12.50	17.50	35.00	150.00	550.00
16,395,000	1869	8.00	12.50	17.50	35.00	150.00	550.00
4,806,000	1870	10.00	14.00	20.00	37.50	175.00	550.00
561,000	1871	35.00	45.00	55.00	85.00	250.00	725.00
6,036,000	1872	9.00	15.00	17.50	30.00	150.00	550.00
4,550,000	1873	9.50	12.50	20.00	35.00	150.00	550.00
3,538,000	1874	11.00	17.50	18.00	40.00	150.00	550.00
2,097,000	1875	12.50	22.50	27.50	50.00	200.00	550.00
2,530,000	1876	12.00	20.00	25.00	40.00	150.00	550.00
?500	1877 only proofs were struck						1750.00
2,350	1878 only proofs were struck						1000.00
29,100	1879	85.00	100.00	135.00	175.00	450.00	750.00
19,955	1880	100.00	135.00	150.00	200.00	500.00	800.00
72,375	1881	85.00	125.00	140.00	200.00	425.00	750.00
11,476,600	1882	9.00	12.50	20.00	30.00	175.00	425.00
1,456,919	1883	10.00	12.50	20.00	30.00	175.00	425.00

LIBERTY HEAD NICKELS

1883   1883–1912

The variety without "CENTS" was issued first, but unscrupulous people goldplated them and passed them off as $5 gold pieces. To remedy the situation, the word "CENTS" was added to the later issues and continued to appear on subsequent dates.

LIBERTY HEAD NICKELS (continued)

QUANTITY	YEAR	GOOD	VERY GOOD	FINE	VERY FINE	EXT. FINE	UNC.	PROOF -63
5,479,519	1883 without "Cents"	$2.25	$3.25	$3.50	$6.00	$9.00	$45.00	$350.00
16,032,983	1883 with "Cents"	6.50	8.50	17.50	25.00	37.50	125.00	300.00
11,273,942	1884	7.00	9.00	18.50	27.50	45.00	150.00	250.00
1,476,490	1885	125.00	200.00	225.00	300.00	400.00	800.00	1100.00
3,330,290	1886	35.00	50.00	75.00	100.00	200.00	400.00	650.00
15,263,652	1887	3.50	5.00	12.50	20.00	40.00	125.00	300.00
10,720,483	1888	6.50	10.00	17.50	22.50	37.50	125.00	300.00
15,881,361	1889	3.50	5.00	12.50	20.00	35.00	110.00	300.00
16,259,272	1890	4.50	6.00	15.00	22.50	37.50	110.00	300.00
16,834,350	1891	3.50	5.00	12.50	20.00	35.00	110.00	300.00
11,699,642	1892	3.50	5.00	12.50	20.00	35.00	110.00	300.00
13,370,195	1893	3.50	5.00	12.50	20.00	35.00	125.00	300.00
5,413,132	1894	7.00	9.00	18.50	27.50	45.00	125.00	300.00
9,979,884	1895	2.50	5.00	12.50	17.50	30.00	125.00	300.00
8,842,920	1896	3.00	6.00	15.00	20.00	25.00	125.00	325.00
20,428,735	1897	1.00	2.00	4.00	7.00	22.50	110.00	300.00
12,532,087	1898	1.00	2.00	4.00	7.00	22.50	110.00	300.00
26,029,031	1899	.75	1.75	4.00	6.50	22.50	110.00	300.00
27,255,995	1900	.75	1.00	3.00	6.00	20.00	100.00	300.00
26,480,213	1901	.75	1.00	3.00	6.00	20.00	100.00	300.00
31,480,579	1902	.75	1.00	3.00	6.00	20.00	100.00	300.00
28,006,725	1903	.75	1.00	3.00	6.00	20.00	100.00	300.00
21,404,984	1904	.75	1.00	3.00	6.00	20.00	100.00	300.00
29,827,276	1905	.75	1.00	3.00	6.00	20.00	100.00	300.00
38,613,725	1906	.75	1.00	3.00	6.00	20.00	100.00	300.00
39,214,800	1907	.75	1.00	3.00	6.00	20.00	100.00	300.00
22,686,177	1908	.75	1.00	3.00	6.00	20.00	100.00	300.00
11,590,526	1909	.75	1.00	3.00	6.00	20.00	100.00	300.00
30,169,353	1910	.75	1.00	3.00	6.00	20.00	100.00	300.00
39,559,372	1911	.75	1.00	3.00	6.00	20.00	100.00	300.00
26,236,714	1912	.75	1.00	3.00	6.00	20.00	100.00	300.00
8,474,000	*1912 D	2.50	3.50	12.50	15.00	50.00	200.00	
238,000	*1912 S	50.00	55.00	100.00	150.00	250.00	650.00	
5 Known	1913 (an outstanding rarity) Sold at an early 1990s public auction for $950,000.00.							

*Mint mark to left of "CENTS" on reverse.

BUFFALO NICKELS

The mint marks are under "Five cents" on the reverse.

1913   1913–1938

QUANTITY	YEAR	GOOD	VERY GOOD	FINE	VERY FINE	EXT. FINE	UNC.
30,993,520	1913 Type 1 —buffalo on mound	$3.00	$3.25	$5.00	$7.00	$12.00	$50.00
2,105,000	1913 S Type 1	7.00	10.00	12.00	20.00	25.00	100.00
5,337,000	1913 D Type 1	4.50	6.00	10.00	12.00	17.50	85.00
29,858,700	1913 Type 2 buffalo on line	2.50	3.50	4.00	5.00	10.00	50.00
1,209,000	1913 S Type 2	50.00	55.00	70.00	90.00	120.00	300.00

BUFFALO NICKELS (continued)

QUANTITY	YEAR	GOOD	VERY GOOD	FINE	VERY FINE	EXT. FINE	UNC.
4,156,000	1913 D						
	Type 2	32.50	37.50	50.00	65.00	75.00	200.00
20,665,738	1914	3.00	4.50	5.50	7.50	12.50	50.00
3,470,000	1914 S	4.50	6.00	8.50	14.00	28.00	100.00
3,912,000	1914 D	20.00	28.00	37.50	50.00	80.00	250.00
20,987,270	1915	1.65	2.50	3.75	5.25	12.00	50.00
1,505,000	1915 S	8.50	12.50	22.50	55.00	75.00	250.00
7,569,500	1915 D	6.00	7.50	15.00	28.00	45.00	120.00
63,498,066	1916	.75	1.00	1.75	3.00	6.50	35.00
11,860,000	1916 S	3.25	4.25	7.00	17.50	37.50	120.00
13,333,000	1916 D	4.25	5.50	9.00	15.00	38.50	115.00
51,424,029	1917	.85	1.00	1.75	3.50	12.00	42.50
4,193,000	1917 S	3.50	6.00	10.00	32.50	57.50	225.00
9,910,800	1917 D	4.00	6.00	11.00	34.00	57.50	215.00
32,086,314	1918	.65	1.25	2.35	5.50	16.00	80.00
4,882,000	1918 S	3.00	6.00	11.00	32.50	65.00	225.00
8,362,000	1918 D	4.00	6.50	12.00	35.00	75.00	285.00
	1918						
	D over 7	275.00	350.00	650.00	1000.00	2400.00	20,000.00
60,868,000	1919	.60	.80	1.50	3.15	8.00	37.50
7,521,000	1919 S	2.50	5.00	10.00	35.00	75.00	275.00
8,006,000	1919 D	3.50	6.50	16.00	45.00	85.00	330.00
63,093,000	1920	.55	.75	1.25	3.00	7.50	42.50
9,689,000	1920 S	1.75	3.00	16.00	27.50	70.00	200.00
9,418,000	1920 D	3.00	5.00	10.00	47.50	75.00	300.00
10,663,000	1921	.90	1.20	3.25	6.25	16.50	80.00
1,557,000	1921 S	12.00	16.50	35.00	100.00	165.00	650.00
35,715,000	1923	.45	.65	1.15	3.00	8.00	40.00
6,142,000	1923 S	1.65	2.50	6.00	22.50	47.50	175.00
21,620,000	1924	.45	.65	1.25	4.00	9.00	55.00
1,437,000	1924 S	4.50	6.50	15.00	120.00	225.00	800.00
5,258,000	1924 D	2.25	3.25	8.00	45.00	70.00	250.00
35,565,100	1925	.45	.70	1.25	3.00	6.50	40.00
6,256,000	1925 S	2.25	4.00	6.00	20.00	50.00	225.00
4,450,000	1925 D	3.50	5.25	12.00	40.00	67.50	275.00
44,693,000	1926	.45	.55	1.00	1.50	5.00	30.00
970,000	1926 S	6.00	8.00	15.00	60.00	300.00	850.00
5,638,000	1926 D	2.00	3.75	9.00	40.00	85.00	175.00
37,981,000	1927	.45	.55	1.00	1.50	5.00	30.00
3,430,000	1927 S	1.10	1.50	4.00	12.50	50.00	175.00
5,730,000	1927 D	1.00	1.50	2.75	12.00	32.50	90.00
23,411,000	1928	.50	.55	1.00	2.25	5.00	30.00
6,936,000	1928 S	.75	1.00	2.00	3.00	12.00	67.50
6,436,000	1928 D	.65	.75	1.50	5.00	12.00	45.00
36,446,000	1929	.40	.55	.90	1.65	3.65	27.50
7,754,000	1929 S	.50	.60	1.00	1.65	7.50	35.00
8,370,000	1929 D	.55	1.00	1.50	3.75	10.00	55.00
22,849,000	1930	.40	.50	1.00	1.65	4.00	30.00
5,435,000	1930 S	.65	.85	1.65	2.00	6.50	55.00
1,200,000	1931 S	3.75	4.50	5.50	7.00	14.00	75.00
20,213,000	1934	.30	.40	.65	1.50	3.75	27.50
7,480,003	1934 D	.50	.60	1.00	2.50	6.50	45.00
58,264,000	1935	.30	.40	.50	.65	1.50	19.00
10,300,000	1935 S	.35	.40	.50	1.25	3.40	25.00
12,092,000	1935 D	.40	.45	.65	2.00	5.00	40.00
119,001,420	1936				1.00	1.75	18.50
14,930,000	1936 S				1.00	2.35	22.00
24,418,000	1936 D				.75	2.25	22.00
79,485,769	1937				.75	1.50	17.50
5,635,000	1937 S				.75	1.75	17.50
17,826,000	1937 D				.75	2.00	17.50
	1937 D three-legged						
	buffalo				200.00	300.00	1250.00
7,020,000	1938 D				1.25	1.75	17.50

JEFFERSON NICKELS

QUANTITY	YEAR	EXT. FINE	UNC.
19,515,365	1938	$.75	$1.75
4,105,000	1938 S	3.50	7.75
5,376,000	1938 D	2.25	6.00
120,627,535	1939	.35	1.35
6,630,000	1939 S	2.50	17.50
3,514,000	1939 D	8.00	35.00
176,499,158	1940	.35	1.00
39,690,000	1940 S	.65	2.00
43,540,000	1940 D	.50	1.75
203,283,720	1941	.40	1.00
43,445,000	1941 S	.50	2.50
53,432,000	1941 D	.50	2.50
49,818,600	1942	.50	2.00
13,938,000	1942 D	2.50	17.50

Wartime Silver Content

QUANTITY	YEAR	EXT. FINE	UNC.
57,900,600	1942 P	4.00	15.00
32,900,000	1942 S	2.50	10.00
271,165,000	1943 P	1.50	4.00
104,060,000	1943 S	1.50	5.00
15,294,000	1943 D	2.50	5.00
119,150,000	1944 P	1.75	4.00
21,640,000	1944 S	2.00	7.50
32,309,000	1944 D	2.00	6.00
119,408,100	1945 P	1.75	4.00
58,939,000	1945 S	1.50	4.00
37,158,000	1945 D	1.50	4.00

The mint marks are to the right of the building or above it on the reverse until 1968, then on the obverse near the date.

Prewar Nickel Content

QUANTITY	YEAR	MS-65
161,116,000	1946	1.00
13,560,000	1946 S	1.75
45,292,200	1946 D	1.00
95,000,000	1947	.75
24,720,000	1947 S	1.50
37,822,000	1947 D	1.25
89,348,000	1948	1.00
11,300,000	1948 S	1.65
44,734,000	1948 D	1.50
60,652,000	1949	1.00
9,716,000	1949 S	3.00
35,238,000	1949 D	1.75
9,847,386	1950	3.00
2,630,030	1950 D	14.00
26,689,500	1951	1.50
7,776,000	1951 S	4.00
20,460,000	1951 D	2.25
64,069,980	1952	.85
20,572,000	1952 S	1.25
30,638,000	1952 D	2.50
46,772,800	1953	.50
19,210,900	1953 S	1.00
59,878,600	1953 D	.85
47,917,350	1954	.35
29,384,000	1954 S	.35
117,183,060	1954 D	.30
8,266,200	1955	1.75
74,464,100	1955 D	.35
35,397,081	1956	.30
67,222,040	1956 D	.30
38,408,000	1957	.30
136,828,900	1957 D	.30
17,088,000	1958	.60
168,249,120	1958 D	.30
27,248,000	1959	.40

QUANTITY	YEAR	MS-65
160,738,240	1959 D	.25
55,416,000	1960	.20
192,582,180	1960 D	.20
76,668,244	1961	.20
229,372,760	1961 D	.20
100,602,019	1962	.20
280,195,720	1962 D	.20
178,851,645	1963	.20
276,829,460	1963 D	.20
1,024,672,000	1964	.20
1,787,297,160	1964 D	.20
133,771,380	1965	.20
153,946,700	1966	.20
107,325,800	1967	.20
91,227,880	1968 D	.20
100,396,001	1968 S	.20
202,807,500	1969 D	.20
120,164,000	1969 S	.20
515,485,380	1970 D	.15
241,464,814	1970 S	.15
106,884,000	1971	.15
316,144,800	1971 D	.15
3,224,138	1971 S (proof only)	
202,036,000	1972	.15
351,694,600	1972 D	.15
3,267,667	1972 S (proof only)	
384,396,000	1973	.15
261,405,400	1973 D	.15
2,769,624	1973 S (proof only)	
601,752,000	1974	.15
277,373,000	1974 D	.15
2,617,350	1974 S (proof only)	
181,772,000	1975	.15
401,875,300	1975 D	.15
	1975 S (proof only)	
367,124,000	1976	.15

JEFFERSON NICKELS (continued)

QUANTITY	YEAR	MS-65	QUANTITY	YEAR	MS-65
563,964,147	1976 D	.15	3,010,497	1986 S (proof only)	
	1976 S (proof only)		371,499,481	1987	.15
585,376,000	1977	.15	410,590,604	1987 D	.15
297,313,422	1977 D	.15	3,792,233	1987 S (proof only)	
	1977 S (proof only)		771,360,000	1988	.15
391,308,000	1978	.15	663,771,652	1988 D	.15
313,092,780	1978 D	.15	3,262,948	1988 S (proof only)	
3,127,781	1978 S (proof only)		898,812,000	1989	.15
463,188,000	1979	.15	570,842,474	1989 D	.15
325,867,672	1979 D	.15	3,215,728	1989 S (proof only)	
3,677,175	1979 S (proof only)		661,636,000	1990	.15
593,004,000	1980	.15	663,938,503	1990 D	.15
502,323,448	1980 D	.15	3,299,559	1990 S (proof only)	
3,554,806	1980 S (proof only)		614,104,000	1991	.15
657,504,000	1981	.15	436,496,678	1991 D	.15
364,801,843	1981 D	.15	2,867,787	1991 S (proof only)	
4,063,083	1981 S (proof only)		399,552,000	1992	.15
292,355,000	1982	.15	450,565,113	1992 D	.15
373,726,544	1982 D	.15	4,176,560	1992 S (proof only)	
3,857,479	1982 S (proof only)		412,076,000	1993	.15
561,615,000	1983	.15	406,084,135	1993 D	.15
536,726,276	1983 D	.15	3,394,792	1993 S (proof only)	
3,228,648	1983 S (proof only)			1994	.15
746,769,000	1984	.15		1994 D	.15
517,675,146	1984 D	.15		1994 S (proof only)	
3,065,110	1984 S (proof only)			1995	.15
647,114,962	1985	.15		1995 D	.15
459,747,446	1985 D	.15		1995 S (proof only)	
3,362,662	1985 S (proof only)				
536,883,493	1986	.15			
61,819,144	1986 D	.15			

Half Dimes

HALF DIMES—FLOWING HAIR TYPE

QUANTITY	YEAR	ABOUT GOOD TO GOOD	VERY GOOD	FINE	VERY FINE
86,416	1794	$325.00	$700.00	$1300.00	$2250.00
	1795	300.00	600.00	1100.00	1600.00

HALF DIMES—DRAPED BUST TYPE

1796–1797 1800–1805

10,230	1796	$400.00	$850.00	$1300.00	$2000.00
	1796 over 5	450.00	1000.00	1400.00	2250.00
44,527	1797 13 stars	350.00	800.00	1200.00	1500.00
	1797 15 stars	325.00	750.00	1100.00	1400.00
	1797 16 stars	325.00	750.00	1100.00	1400.00
24,000	1800	225.00	500.00	750.00	1100.00

QUANTITY	YEAR	ABOUT GOOD TO GOOD	VERY GOOD	FINE	VERY FINE
	1800 LIBERTY	225.00	500.00	750.00	1100.00
33,910	1801	225.00	500.00	750.00	1100.00
13,010	1802 extremely rare	2250.00	5000.00	15,000.00	25,000.00
37,850	1803	225.00	500.00	750.00	1000.00
15,600	1805	250.00	650.00	950.00	1650.00

HALF DIMES—CAPPED BUST TYPE

QUANTITY	YEAR	GOOD TO VERY GOOD	FINE	VERY FINE	EXT. FINE	UNC.
1,230,000	1829	$20.00	$27.50	$40.00	$85.00	$500.00
1,240,000	1830	20.00	27.50	40.00	80.00	450.00
1,242,700	1831	20.00	27.50	40.00	80.00	450.00
965,000	1832	20.00	27.50	40.00	80.00	450.00
1,370,000	1833	20.00	27.50	40.00	80.00	450.00
1,480,000	1834	20.00	27.50	40.00	80.00	450.00
2,760,000	1835	20.00	27.50	40.00	80.00	450.00
1,900,000	1836	20.00	27.50	40.00	80.00	450.00
2,276,000	1837 large 5c	20.00	27.50	40.00	80.00	450.00
	1837 small 5c	27.50	60.00	85.00	200.00	1750.00

1837–1838   **1838–1859**

The mint marks are under the wreath, or within it, on the reverse.

HALF DIMES—LIBERTY SEATED TYPE

		Without stars			
2,255,000	1837	$45.00	$75.00	$100.00	$225.00	$850.00
?	1838 O	55.00	120.00	250.00	650.00	3000.00
		With stars, no drapery from elbow			
2,255,000	1838	8.00	12.00	25.00	55.00	450.00
1,069,150	1839	8.00	12.00	25.00	55.00	450.00
1,096,550	1839 O	9.00	15.00	30.00	65.00	500.00
1,344,085	**1840	8.00	12.00	25.00	55.00	450.00
935,000	**1840 O	10.00	20.00	40.00	85.00	550.00
		With drapery from elbow			
	1840	12.50	17.50	40.00	100.00	700.00
	1840 O	20.00	35.00	60.00	125.00	850.00
1,150,000	1841	7.50	12.00	20.00	50.00	375.00
815,000	1841 O	10.00	17.50	35.00	70.00	550.00
815,000	1842	8.00	12.00	22.00	50.00	340.00
350,000	1842 O	12.00	25.00	75.00	150.00	750.00
1,165,000	1843	8.00	12.00	25.00	50.00	340.00
430,000	1844	8.00	15.00	25.00	50.00	375.00
220,000	1844 O	30.00	75.00	225.00	500.00	1000.00
1,564,000	1845	8.00	12.00	25.00	45.00	340.00

**Includes 1840 half dimes with drapery from elbow

HALF DIMES—LIBERTY SEATED TYPE (continued)

QUANTITY	YEAR	GOOD TO VERY GOOD	FINE	VERY FINE	EXT. FINE	UNC.
27,000	1846	85.00	250.00	400.00	800.00	1750.00
1,274,000	1847	8.00	12.00	25.00	45.00	340.00
668,000	1848	8.00	12.00	25.00	45.00	340.00
600,000	1848 O	12.00	25.00	55.00	90.00	575.00
1,309,000	1849	8.00	12.00	25.00	45.00	340.00
	1849 over 48	10.00	15.00	35.00	65.00	450.00
140,000	1849 O	35.00	67.50	150.00	365.00	1200.00
955,000	1850	8.00	12.00	25.00	50.00	300.00
690,000	1850 O	10.00	20.00	55.00	100.00	700.00
781,000	1851	8.00	12.00	25.00	50.00	375.00
860,000	1851 O	10.00	20.00	50.00	75.00	675.00
1,000,500	1852	8.00	12.00	25.00	50.00	375.00
260,000	1852 O	15.00	40.00	75.00	200.00	1250.00
13,345,020	1853 no arrows	17.50	45.00	80.00	150.00	650.00
	1853 arrows	8.00	12.00	20.00	50.00	300.00
2,360,000	1853 O no arrows	100.00	175.00	300.00	600.00	2500.00
	1853 O arrows	8.00	10.00	25.00	50.00	475.00
5,740,000	1854 arrows	8.00	10.00	25.00	50.00	300.00
1,560,000	1854 O arrows	8.00	12.00	30.00	60.00	500.00
1,750,000	1855 arrows	8.00	10.00	25.00	40.00	475.00
600,000	1855 O arrows	10.00	20.00	50.00	90.00	650.00
4,880,000	1856	7.00	10.00	20.00	40.00	300.00
1,100,000	1856 O	7.00	10.00	20.00	45.00	500.00
1,380,000	1857 O	7.00	10.00	20.00	50.00	500.00
3,500,000	1858	7.00	10.00	20.00	40.00	275.00
1,660,000	1858 O	7.00	10.00	20.00	45.00	400.00
340,000	1859	10.00	17.50	35.00	65.00	350.00
560,000	1859 O	7.00	12.50	27.50	65.00	415.00

1860–1873

QUANTITY	YEAR	GOOD TO VERY GOOD	FINE	VERY FINE	EXT. FINE	UNC.
799,000	1860 no stars	7.50	11.00	15.00	35.00	300.00
1,060,000	1860 O	7.50	12.50	20.00	50.00	350.00
3,281,000	1861	7.50	11.00	15.00	35.00	315.00
1,492,550	1862	7.50	11.00	15.00	35.00	315.00
18,460	1863	37.50	75.00	135.00	200.00	700.00
100,000	1863 S	20.00	30.00	50.00	115.00	675.00
48,470	1864	200.00	300.00	350.00	500.00	1500.00
90,000	1864 S	25.00	65.00	85.00	165.00	825.00
13,500	1865	75.00	125.00	215.00	315.00	1000.00
120,000	1865 S	15.00	25.00	50.00	100.00	700.00
10,725	1866	55.00	125.00	200.00	325.00	800.00
120,000	1866 S	15.00	30.00	50.00	115.00	700.00
8,625	1867	80.00	150.00	275.00	350.00	1000.00
120,000	1867 S	14.00	32.50	55.00	140.00	625.00
85,900	1868	15.00	35.00	60.00	150.00	650.00
280,000	1868 S	8.00	15.00	25.00	50.00	450.00
208,600	1869	8.00	15.00	22.50	45.00	400.00
230,000	1869 S	8.00	12.00	20.00	45.00	400.00
536,600	1870	6.50	10.00	15.00	35.00	340.00
1,488,860	1871	6.50	10.00	15.00	30.00	300.00
161,000	1871 S	17.50	30.00	65.00	110.00	450.00
2,947,950	1872	6.50	9.00	15.00	30.00	275.00
837,000	1872 S in wreath	6.50	9.00	15.00	32.50	285.00
	1872 S below wreath	6.50	9.00	15.00	32.50	285.00
712,600	1873	6.50	9.00	15.00	32.50	285.00
324,000	1873 S	6.50	9.00	15.00	32.50	285.00

Dimes

DIMES—DRAPED BUST TYPE

1795–1797   **1798–1807**

QUANTITY	YEAR	ABOUT GOOD TO GOOD	VERY GOOD	FINE	VERY FINE
22,135	1796	$550.00	$1250.00	$1850.00	$2750.00
25,261	1797 13 stars	425.00	1100.00	1350.00	2150.00
	1797 16 stars	450.00	1150.00	1400.00	2350.00
27,550	1798 over 97	225.00	475.00	900.00	1275.00
	1798	225.00	475.00	900.00	1275.00
21,760	1800	200.00	450.00	850.00	1000.00
34,640	1801	225.00	500.00	1000.00	1250.00
10,975	1802	235.00	550.00	1000.00	1350.00
33,040	1803	225.00	500.00	900.00	1200.00
8,265	1804	325.00	550.00	1500.00	3250.00
120,780	1805	175.00	425.00	800.00	1000.00
165,000	1807	175.00	425.00	800.00	1000.00

DIMES—CAPPED BUST TYPE

QUANTITY	YEAR	ABOUT GOOD TO GOOD	VERY GOOD	FINE	VERY FINE	UNC.
44,710	1809	$50.00	$125.00	$225.00	$425.00	$3800.00
65,180	1811 over 09	35.00	75.00	100.00	215.00	3350.00
421,500	1814	25.00	40.00	55.00	100.00	2500.00
942,587	1820	22.50	32.50	50.00	80.00	1800.00
1,186,512	1821	22.50	30.00	45.00	75.00	1750.00
100,000	1822	100.00	150.00	300.00	500.00	6500.00
440,000	1823 over 22	25.00	35.00	50.00	80.00	2250.00
?	1824 over 22	22.50	40.00	65.00	100.00	2250.00
510,000	1825	25.00	32.50	50.00	80.00	1400.00
1,215,000	1827	15.00	32.50	45.00	75.00	1400.00
125,000	1828 large date	30.00	50.00	75.00	125.00	1750.00
	1828 small date	25.00	35.00	55.00	80.00	1750.00
	1829 large 10c	22.50	40.00	60.00	140.00	1100.00
	1829 medium 10c	17.50	35.00	45.00	125.00	1050.00
	1829 small 10c	17.50	35.00	45.00	125.00	1050.00
510,000	1830	17.50	35.00	50.00	125.00	850.00
771,350	1831	17.50	35.00	45.00	125.00	800.00
522,500	1832	17.50	35.00	45.00	125.00	800.00
485,000	1833	17.50	35.00	45.00	125.00	800.00
635,000	1834	17.50	35.00	45.00	125.00	800.00
1,410,000	1835	17.50	35.00	45.00	125.00	800.00
1,190,000	1836	17.50	35.00	45.00	125.00	800.00
1,042,000	* 1837	17.50	35.00	45.00	125.00	800.00

*Includes Liberty Seated dimes of 1837

DIMES—LIBERTY SEATED TYPE

1837–1838   **1838–1860**

The mint marks are under the wreath or within it, on the reverse.

QUANTITY	YEAR	GOOD TO VERY GOOD	FINE	VERY FINE	EXT. FINE	UNC.
			Without stars			
	1837	$42.50	$80.00	$135.00	$300.00	$1100.00
402,434	1838 O	50.00	120.00	200.00	350.00	2250.00
		With stars, no drapery from elbow				
1,992,500	1838	17.50	32.50	50.00	125.00	1000.00
1,053,115	1839	7.50	15.00	25.00	60.00	425.00
1,243,272	1839 O	8.00	20.00	35.00	55.00	500.00
1,358,580	**1840	7.50	14.00	25.00	55.00	425.00
1,175,000	1840 O	8.50	20.00	35.00	65.00	850.00
	1841 very rare					

**Includes 1840 dimes with drapery from elbow

QUANTITY	YEAR	GOOD TO VERY GOOD	FINE	VERY FINE	EXT. FINE	UNC.
		With drapery from elbow				
	1840	17.50	35.00	55.00	120.00	800.00
1,622,500	1841	6.00	10.00	25.00	50.00	350.00
2,007,500	1841 O	7.50	15.00	25.00	50.00	500.00
1,887,500	1842	6.00	10.00	20.00	45.00	450.00
2,020,000	1842 O	10.00	20.00	30.00	80.00	550.00
1,370,000	1843	6.00	10.00	20.00	45.00	450.00
150,000	1843 O	40.00	110.00	350.00	600.00	2000.00
72,500	1844	40.00	80.00	160.00	375.00	1750.00
1,755,000	1845	6.00	10.00	20.00	35.00	400.00
230,000	1845 O	37.50	100.00	160.00	500.00	2000.00
31,300	1846	65.00	120.00	200.00	425.00	850.00
245,000	1847	12.50	20.00	45.00	90.00	1000.00
451,500	1848	9.00	17.50	35.00	75.00	500.00
839,000	1849	6.00	12.00	25.00	75.00	600.00
300,000	1849 O	15.00	30.00	65.00	200.00	2000.00
1,931,500	1850	6.00	12.00	25.00	45.00	400.00
510,000	1850 O	15.00	30.00	55.00	125.00	1200.00
1,026,500	1851	6.00	12.00	25.00	50.00	425.00
400,000	1851 O	12.50	20.00	45.00	150.00	1250.00
1,535,500	1852	6.00	12.00	20.00	45.00	450.00
430,000	1852 O	15.00	30.00	50.00	200.00	1500.00
12,173,010	††1853	30.00	55.00	85.00	175.00	1000.00

†† Includes 1853 dimes with arrows at date

QUANTITY	YEAR	GOOD TO VERY GOOD	FINE	VERY FINE	EXT. FINE	UNC.
		With arrows at date				
	1853	5.50	12.00	25.00	50.00	400.00
1,100,000	1853 O	8.00	15.00	35.00	80.00	800.00
4,470,000	1854	6.00	12.00	22.50	45.00	475.00
1,770,000	1854 O	6.50	17.50	27.50	50.00	500.00
2,075,000	1855	6.00	12.00	22.50	45.00	475.00
		Without arrows at date				
5,780,000	1856	5.50	12.00	20.00	35.00	400.00
1,180,000	1856 O	5.50	12.00	20.00	35.00	550.00
70,000	1856 S	40.00	80.00	125.00	500.00	2500.00
5,580,000	1857	5.50	12.00	20.00	25.00	350.00
1,540,000	1857 O	5.50	12.50	25.00	40.00	475.00
1,540,000	1858	5.50	12.00	20.00	35.00	350.00
290,000	1858 O	10.00	25.00	40.00	75.00	700.00
60,000	1858 S	45.00	85.00	150.00	400.00	1250.00
430,000	1859	5.50	12.00	20.00	35.00	425.00
480,000	1859 O	5.50	12.50	25.00	45.00	450.00

1860–1891

QUANTITY	YEAR	GOOD TO VERY GOOD	FINE	VERY FINE	EXT. FINE	UNC.
140,000	1860 S	17.50	45.00	125.00	225.00	1000.00
607,000	1860	$5.50	$12.00	$15.00	$27.50	$275.00
40,000	1860 O rare	450.00	750.00	1000.00	2500.00	11,000.00
1,924,000	1861	5.50	12.00	15.00	27.50	275.00
172,500	1861 S	16.00	35.00	70.00	150.00	1000.00
847,550	1862	5.50	12.00	15.00	27.50	265.00
180,750	1862 S	15.00	37.50	65.00	135.00	1000.00
14,460	1863	50.00	100.00	175.00	300.00	1000.00
157,500	1863 S	20.00	40.00	75.00	165.00	1000.00
11,470	1864	55.00	115.00	150.00	275.00	1000.00
230,000	1864 S	55.00	30.00	55.00	140.00	1050.00
10,500	1865	15.00	125.00	225.00	325.00	1100.00
175,000	1865 S	15.00	32.50	65.00	175.00	1000.00
8,725	1866	90.00	225.00	300.00	500.00	1300.00
135,000	1866 S	15.00	35.00	60.00	150.00	1100.00
6,625	1867	175.00	300.00	500.00	625.00	1500.00
140,000	1867 S	15.00	35.00	55.00	140.00	1100.00
466,250	1868	5.50	12.50	25.00	55.00	500.00
260,000	1868 S	12.00	25.00	45.00	75.00	425.00
256,600	1869	5.50	12.00	17.50	40.00	450.00
450,000	1869 S	12.00	25.00	35.00	100.00	425.00
471,500	1870	5.50	12.00	15.00	35.00	400.00
50,000	1870 S	70.00	125.00	200.00	350.00	2750.00
753,610	1871	5.50	12.00	15.00	35.00	300.00
320,000	1871 S	12.50	30.00	60.00	125.00	1000.00
20,100	1871 CC rare	275.00	750.00	1000.00	2000.00	6500.00
2,396,450	1872	5.50	12.00	15.00	35.00	275.00
190,000	1872 S	12.50	30.00	60.00	125.00	800.00
24,000	1872 CC	150.00	450.00	675.00	1200.00	3500.00
3,947,100	1873 no arrows	5.50	12.00	15.00	40.00	300.00
	1873 arrows	12.50	30.00	45.00	100.00	750.00
455,000	1873 S arrows	20.00	45.00	65.00	110.00	750.00
31,191	1873 CC arrows	425.00	800.00	1000.00	1750.00	22,500.00
	1873 CC no arrows					(unique)
2,940,700	1874 arrows	15.00	135.00	50.00	100.00	750.00
240,000	1874 S arrows	22.50	50.00	80.00	140.00	850.00
10,817	1874 CC arrows (very rare)	325.00	1250.00	2000.00	4250.00	22,500.00

Without arrows at date

QUANTITY	YEAR	GOOD TO VERY GOOD	FINE	VERY FINE	EXT. FINE	UNC.
10,350,700	1875	5.50	12.00	15.00	30.00	235.00
9,070,000	1875 S in wreath	5.50	12.00	15.00	30.00	235.00
	1875 S below wreath	5.50	12.00	15.00	30.00	235.00
4,645,000	1875 CC in wreath	5.50	12.00	15.00	30.00	275.00
	1875 CC below wreath	5.50	12.50	17.50	35.00	300.00
11,461,150	1876	5.50	9.00	12.50	30.00	225.00
10,420,000	1876 S	5.50	9.00	12.50	30.00	225.00
8,270,000	1876 CC	5.50	9.00	12.50	30.00	250.00
7,310,510	1877	5.50	9.00	12.50	30.00	225.00
2,340,000	1877 S	5.50	9.00	12.50	30.00	225.00

DIMES—LIBERTY SEATED TYPE (continued)

QUANTITY	YEAR	GOOD TO VERY GOOD	VERY FINE	EXT. FINE	FINE	UNC.
7,700,000	1877 CC	5.50	10.00	15.00	35.00	325.00
1,678,800	1878	5.50	10.00	12.50	32.50	250.00
200,000	1878 CC	22.50	50.00	85.00	150.00	675.00
15,100	1879	65.00	100.00	200.00	300.00	725.00
37,355	1880	45.00	85.00	175.00	200.00	550.00
24,975	1881	50.00	90.00	185.00	225.00	575.00
3,911,100	1882	5.50	9.00	12.50	30.00	250.00
7,675,712	1883	5.50	9.00	12.50	30.00	250.00
3,366,380	1884	5.50	9.00	12.50	30.00	250.00
564,969	1884 S	11.00	22.50	40.00	75.00	400.00
2,533,427	1885	5.50	9.00	12.50	30.00	235.00
43,690	1885 S	200.00	300.00	400.00	625.00	3750.00
6,377,570	1886	5.50	9.00	12.50	30.00	225.00
206,524	1886 S	11.00	27.50	50.00	80.00	500.00
11,283,939	1887	5.50	9.00	12.50	30.00	225.00
4,454,450	1887 S	5.50	9.00	12.50	30.00	235.00
5,496,487	1888	5.50	9.00	12.50	30.00	225.00
1,720,000	1888 S	5.50	9.00	15.00	35.00	235.00
7,380,711	1889	5.50	9.00	12.50	30.00	225.00
972,678	1889 S	11.00	25.00	60.00	90.00	400.00
9,911,541	1890	5.50	9.00	12.50	30.00	225.00
1,423,076	1890 S	5.50	9.00	15.00	32.50	275.00
15,310,600	1891	5.50	9.00	12.50	30.00	225.00
4,540,000	1891 O	5.50	9.00	15.00	35.00	275.00
3,196,116	1891 S	5.50	9.00	12.50	30.00	275.00

DIMES—LIBERTY HEAD TYPE

The mint marks are under the wreath on the reverse.

QUANTITY	YEAR	GOOD	VERY GOOD	FINE	VERY FINE	EXT. FINE	UNC.	PROOF
12,121,245	1892	$2.00	$3.75	$5.75	$10.00	$25.00	$150.00	$750.00
3,841,700	1892 O	4.50	8.00	10.00	17.50	30.00	200.00	
990,710	1892 S	25.00	35.00	45.00	60.00	90.00	325.00	
3,340,792	1893	4.00	6.00	9.00	15.00	25.00	200.00	825.00
1,760,000	1893 O	12.00	17.50	25.00	35.00	50.00	275.00	
2,491,401	1893 S	5.50	7.00	13.50	20.00	35.00	275.00	
1,330,972	1894	7.00	10.00	15.00	25.00	35.00	225.00	825.00
720,000	1894 O	30.00	42.50	70.00	100.00	200.00	1000.00	
24	*1894 S ext. rare						100,000.00*	
690,880	1895	35.00	50.00	80.00	100.00	150.00	450.00	825.00
440,000	1895 O	100.00	125.00	200.00	300.00	375.00	1750.00	
1,120,000	1895 S	13.50	20.00	27.50	40.00	65.00	350.00	
2,000,762	1896	5.50	8.00	12.50	20.00	32.50	215.00	650.00
610,000	1896 O	40.00	50.00	70.00	90.00	150.00	500.00	
575,056	1896 S	32.50	45.00	65.00	100.00	200.00	725.00	
10,869,264	1897	1.50	2.25	5.50	8.00	20.00	175.00	625.00
666,000	1897 O	32.50	40.00	60.00	80.00	175.00	625.00	
1,342,844	1897 S	7.50	13.50	22.50	37.50	60.00	275.00	
16,320,735	1898	1.50	2.00	4.25	7.50	17.50	175.00	625.00
2,130,000	1898 O	4.00	6.25	12.50	27.50	55.00	250.00	
1,702,507	1898 S	4.00	6.25	12.50	25.00	50.00	225.00	
19,580,846	1899	1.35	1.75	4.25	10.00	20.00	165.00	625.00
2,650,000	1899 O	3.75	7.00	15.00	25.00	50.00	250.00	
1,867,493	1899 S	4.00	6.50	12.50	20.00	40.00	250.00	

QUANTITY	YEAR	GOOD	VERY GOOD	FINE	VERY FINE	EXT. FINE	UNC.	PROOF
17,600,912	1900	1.25	2.00	5.00	7.00	17.50	125.00	625.00
2,010,000	1900 O	5.00	8.00	15.00	25.00	55.00	250.00	
5,168,270	1900 S	2.00	3.25	6.00	10.00	22.50	150.00	
18,860,478	1901	1.25	1.50	3.50	7.00	15.00	150.00	625.00
5,620,000	1901 O	1.85	3.25	7.00	15.00	40.00	375.00	
593,022	1901 S	30.00	55.00	85.00	125.00	190.00	750.00	
21,380,777	1902	1.25	2.00	4.25	10.00	20.00	175.00	625.00
4,500,000	1902 O	1.75	3.25	7.00	15.00	30.00	235.00	
2,070,000	1902 S	3.50	7.00	12.50	25.00	50.00	275.00	
19,500,755	1903	1.50	1.75	5.00	10.00	20.00	175.00	625.00
8,180,000	1903 O	1.75	2.75	6.50	12.50	27.50	225.00	
613,300	1903 S	25.00	35.00	55.00	70.00	135.00	575.00	
14,601,027	1904	1.35	1.75	5.25	10.00	25.00	175.00	625.00
800,000	1904 S	17.50	27.50	40.00	55.00	90.00	575.00	
14,552,350	1905	1.25	1.50	5.00	10.00	17.50	175.00	625.00
3,400,000	1905 O	1.75	3.75	10.00	15.00	35.00	225.00	
6,855,199	1905 S	1.50	2.50	5.50	12.00	25.00	225.00	
19,958,406	1906	1.25	1.50	3.00	8.00	17.50	175.00	625.00
4,060,000	1906 D	1.50	2.50	7.00	12.50	25.00	185.00	
2,610,000	1906 O	2.65	5.50	12.50	22.50	32.50	175.00	
3,136,640	1906 S	2.00	3.75	7.50	12.50	30.00	175.00	625.00
22,220,575	1907	1.25	1.75	3.00	9.00	20.00	175.00	
4,080,000	1907 D	1.50	3.50	7.00	12.50	30.00	175.00	
5,058,000	1907 O	1.50	2.75	6.50	12.00	27.50	185.00	
3,178,470	1907 S	1.50	2.75	7.00	12.50	27.50	185.00	625.00
10,600,545	1908	1.25	1.50	3.75	10.00	25.00	175.00	
7,490,000	1908 D	1.25	1.75	3.50	9.00	22.50	175.00	
1,789,000	1908 O	3.50	6.50	12.50	20.00	35.00	200.00	
3,220,000	1908 S	1.50	2.75	7.00	12.00	25.00	180.00	625.00
10,240,650	1909	1.25	1.75	3.50	10.00	22.50	175.00	
954,000	1909 D	3.75	6.50	14.00	27.50	50.00	225.00	
2,287,000	1909 O	2.75	3.75	9.00	17.50	32.50	235.00	
1,000,000	1909 S	4.25	7.75	17.50	35.00	55.00	235.00	625.00
11,520,551	1910	1.35	1.65	3.00	9.00	22.50	175.00	
3,490,000	1910 D	1.65	2.50	5.00	11.00	27.50	200.00	
1,240,000	1910 S	2.50	4.25	7.75	17.50	32.50	225.00	625.00
18,870,543	1911	1.25	1.75	3.00	7.50	22.50	175.00	
11,209,000	1911 D	1.25	1.40	3.00	7.50	22.50	175.00	
3,520,000	1911 S	1.50	2.25	3.75	11.00	27.50	185.00	625.00
19,350,700	1912	1.25	1.75	2.75	7.50	27.50	175.00	
11,760,000	1912 D	1.35	1.75	2.75	7.50	27.50	175.00	
3,420,000	1912 S	1.75	2.35	4.25	7.75	25.00	185.00	625.00
19,760,622	1913	1.25	1.65	2.75	6.75	22.50	175.00	
510,000	1913 S	7.50	13.00	27.50	45.00	90.00	300.00	700.00
17,360,655	1914	1.25	1.75	2.75	7.50	22.50	175.00	
11,908,000	1914 D	1.25	1.75	2.75	7.50	22.50	175.00	
2,100,000	1914 S	1.75	2.75	7.00	11.00	27.50	185.00	700.00
5,620,450	1915	1.25	1.75	3.75	10.00	22.50	175.00	
960,000	1915 S	2.50	3.25	10.00	16.50	32.50	190.00	
18,490,000	1916	1.25	1.75	3.25	9.00	22.50	175.00	
5,820,000	1916 S	1.25	1.75	3.25	9.00	22.50	175.00	

*A Proof specimen fetched $275,000.00 at a 1/16/90 auction.

DIMES—MERCURY HEAD TYPE

The mint marks are to the left of the fasces on the reverse.

DIMES—MERCURY HEAD TYPE (continued)

QUANTITY	YEAR	GOOD	VERY GOOD	FINE	VERY FINE	EXT. FINE	UNC.
22,180,080	1916	$1.00	$2.50	$3.50	$5.50	$7.50	$35.00
264,0000	1916 D	275.00	350.00	800.00	1250.00	2000.00	3750.00
10,450,000	1916 S	2.75	3.75	5.50	7.00	13.50	37.50
55,230,000	1917	1.20	1.35	1.75	2.50	6.25	30.00
9,402,000	1917 D	2.15	4.50	7.75	12.00	30.00	125.00
27,330,000	1917 S	1.25	1.65	2.00	3.50	7.25	65.00
26,680,000	1918	1.10	1.35	3.75	7.50	20.00	70.00
22,674,800	1918 D	1.25	1.50	4.25	8.00	16.50	100.00
19,300,000	1918 S	1.10	1.35	2.35	7.00	16.50	80.00
35,740,000	1919	1.00	1.25	2.00	3.25	7.50	45.00
9,939,000	1919 D	1.75	3.00	8.00	15.00	32.50	125.00
8,850,000	1919 S	1.75	3.25	8.00	15.00	32.50	135.00
59,030,000	1920	1.00	1.50	1.50	1.75	4.00	30.00
19,171,000	1920 D	1.10	1.65	2.15	4.75	11.00	80.00
13,820,000	1920 S	1.10	1.25	2.00	4.50	12.00	80.00
1,230,000	1921	16.50	25.00	50.00	90.00	350.00	900.00
1,080,000	1921 D	27.50	40.00	75.00	150.00	400.00	850.00
50,130,000	1923	1.00	1.10	1.20	1.50	3.50	25.00
6,440,000	1923 S	1.10	1.50	3.75	6.50	25.00	100.00
24,010,000	1924	1.00	1.10	1.25	2.00	5.00	50.00
6,810,000	1924 D	1.10	1.65	3.75	5.50	18.00	110.00
7,120,000	1924 S	1.00	1.35	2.50	5.50	18.00	100.00
25,610,000	1925	1.00	1.15	1.35	2.00	5.00	50.00
5,117,000	1925 D	2.25	4.25	9.00	22.50	70.00	250.00
5,850,000	1925 S	1.10	1.35	2.00	6.25	22.50	125.00
32,160,000	1926	1.00	1.15	1.30	1.50	4.00	25.00
6,828,000	1926 D	1.10	1.50	2.50	5.00	15.00	80.00
1,520,000	1926 S	6.50	8.50	16.50	22.50	125.00	625.00
28,080,000	1927	1.00	1.15	1.25	1.50	3.50	25.00
4,812,000	1927 D	1.15	2.75	5.50	20.00	35.00	200.00
4,770,000	1927 S	1.10	1.35	2.00	5.50	17.50	150.00
19,480,000	1928	1.00	1.15	1.25	1.50	3.50	35.00
4,161,000	1928 D	1.25	2.50	4.00	15.00	35.00	125.00
7,400,000	1928 S	1.10	1.25	1.50	3.75	11.00	75.00
25,970,000	1929	1.00	1.10	1.20	1.40	3.00	25.00
5,034,000	1929 D	1.10	1.25	2.40	3.25	6.50	30.00
4,730,000	1929 S	1.00	1.15	1.65	2.75	4.25	50.00
6,770,000	1930	1.00	1.15	1.50	1.75	4.50	40.00
1,843,000	1930 S	2.25	3.00	4.00	5.00	15.00	150.00
3,150,000	1931	1.20	1.30	1.75	3.25	7.25	60.00
1,260,000	1931 D	7.00	8.00	9.00	14.00	22.50	125.00
1,800,000	1931 S	2.25	3.50	4.00	4.75	12.50	85.00
24,080,000	1934	1.00	1.15	1.35	1.40	4.00	32.50
6,772,000	1934 D	1.00	1.30	1.50	2.00	6.00	75.00
58,830,000	1935	1.00	1.10	1.20	1.30	1.75	20.00
10,477,000	1935 D	1.00	1.15	1.30	2.00	7.00	40.00
15,840,000	1935 S	1.00	1.10	1.20	1.30	2.25	25.00
87,504,130	1936				1.25	1.50	12.50
16,132,000	1936 D				1.35	5.00	30.00
9,210,000	1936 S				1.25	2.75	20.00
56,865,756	1937				1.00	1.50	12.00
14,146,000	1937 D				1.10	1.50	40.00
9,740,000	1937 S				1.10	1.50	25.00
22,198,728	1938				1.00	1.40	12.50
5,537,000	1938 D				1.25	2.25	22.50
8,090,000	1938 S				1.25	2.25	20.00
67,749,321	1939				1.10	1.65	10.00
24,394,000	1939 D				1.10	1.65	12.50
10,540,000	1939 S				1.35	3.00	25.00
65,361,827	1940				1.10	1.50	8.00
21,198,000	1940 D				1.10	1.50	15.00
21,560,000	1940 S				1.10	1.50	12.50
175,106,557	1941				1.10	1.50	8.00
45,634,000	1941 D				1.10	1.50	15.00
43,090,000	1941 S				1.10	1.50	12.50

1942

The 1942/41 dime very clearly shows the numeral "1" at the front edge of the "2" in the date. The second "1" is close to the "4" as on the regular 1941 dimes.

QUANTITY	YEAR	VERY FINE	EXT. FINE	UNC.
205,432,329	1942 over 1	275.00	350.00	1250.00
	1942			7.50
60,740,000	1942 D	1.10	1.50	12.50
49,300,000	1942 S	1.10	1.50	17.50
191,710,000	1943	1.10	1.50	6.00
71,949,000	1943 D	1.10	1.50	6.00
60,400,000	1943 S	1.10	1.50	10.00
231,410,000	1944	1.10	1.50	6.00
62,224,000	1944 D	1.10	1.50	6.00
49,490,000	1944 S	1.10	1.50	6.00
159,130,000	1945	1.10	1.50	6.00
40,245,000	1945 D	1.10	1.50	11.00
41,920,000	1945 S	1.10	1.50	15.00

DIMES—ROOSEVELT TYPE

QUANTITY	YEAR	EXT. FINE	MS-63
255,250,000	1946	$1.15	$2.00
61,043,500	1946 D	1.15	2.50
27,900,000	1946 S	1.15	3.50
121,520,000	1947	1.15	2.50
46,835,000	1947 D	1.15	5.00
38,840,000	1947 S	1.15	4.00

The mint marks are at the left bottom of the torch on the reverse.

QUANTITY	YEAR	MS-65	QUANTITY	YEAR	MS-65
74,950,000	1948	3.50	85,780,000	1959	1.25
52,841,000	1948 D	3.50	164,919,790	1959 D	1.25
35,520,000	1948 S	5.00	70,390,000	1960	1.25
30,940,000	194	17.50	200,160,400	1960 D	1.25
26,034,000	1949 D	8.00	96,758,244	1961	1.25
13,510,000	1949 S	25.00	209,146,550	1961 D	1.25
50,181,500	1950	3.50	75,668,019	1962	1.25
46,803,000	1950 D	3.00	334,948,380	1962 D	1.25
20,440,000	1950 S	15.00	126,725,645	1963	1.25
103,937,602	1951	2.50	421,476,530	1963 D	1.25
52,191,800	1951 D	2.00	929,360,000	1964	1.25
31,630,000	1951 S	10.00	1,357,517,180	1964 D	1.25
99,122,073	1952	2.50	1,649,780,570	1965	.25
122,100,000	1952 D	2.50	1,380,474,957	1966	.25
44,419,500	1952 S	5.00	2,244,007,320	1967	.25
53,618,920	1953	2.00	424,470,400	1968	.25
136,400,000	1953 D	1.75	480,748,280	1968 D	.25
39,180,000	1953 S	2.75	3,041,509	1968 S (proof only)	
114,243,503	1954	2.00	145,790,000	1969	.25
106,397,000	1954 D	2.00	563,323,870	1969 D	.25
22,860,000	1954 S	2.00	2,934,631	1969 S (proof only)	
12,828,381	1955	2.50	345,570,000	1970	.25
13,959,000	1955 D	1.75	754,942,100	1970 D	.25
18,510,000	1955 S	1.75	2,632,810	1970 S (proof only)	
108,821,081	1956	1.50	162,690,000	1971	.25
108,015,100	1956 D	1.50	377,914,240	1971 D	.25
160,160,000	1957	1.50	3,244,138	1971 S (proof only)	
113,354,330	1957 D	1.50	431,540,000	1972	.25
31,910,000	1958	1.75	330,290,000	1972 D	.25
136,564,600	1958 D	1.25	3,267,667	1972 S (proof only)	

DIMES—ROOSEVELT TYPE (continued)

QUANTITY	YEAR	MS-65	QUANTITY	YEAR	MS-65
315,670,000	1973	.25	473,326,974	1986 D	.20
455,032,426	1973 D	.25	3,010,497	1986 S (proof only)	
2,769,624	1973 S (proof only)		762,709,481	1987	.20
470,248,000	1974	.25	653,203,402	1987 D	.20
571,083,000	1974 D	.25	3,792,233	1987 S (proof only)	
2,617,350	1974 S (proof only)		1,030,550,000	1988	.20
585,673,900	1975	.25	962,385,489	1988 D	.20
313,705,300	1975 D	.25	3,262,938	1988 S (proof only)	
2,845,450	1975 S (proof only)		1,298,400,000	1989	.20
568,760,000	1976	.25	896,535,597	1989 D	.20
695,222,774	1976 D	.25	3,215,728	1989 S (proof only)	
4,149,730	1976 (proof only)		1,034,340,000	1990	.20
796,930,000	1977	.25	839,995,824	1990 D	.20
376,607,228	1977 D	.25	3,299,559	1990 S (proof only)	
3,251,152	1977 S (proof only)		927,220,000	1991	.20
663,980,000	1978	.20	601,241,114	1991 D	.20
282,847,540	1978 D	.20	2,867,787	1991 S (proof only)	
3,127,781	1978 S (proof only)		593,500,000	1992	.20
315,440,000	1979	.20	616,273,932	1992 D	.20
390,921,184	1979 D	.20	2,858,981	1992 S (proof only)	
3,677,175	1979 S (proof only)		766,180,000	1993	.20
735,170,000	1980	.20	750,110,166	1993D	.20
719,354,321	1980 D	.20	2,633,439	1993S (proof only)	
3,554,806	1980 S (proof only)			1994	.20
676,650,000	1981	.20		1994 D	.20
712,284,143	1981 D	.20		1994 S (proof only)	
4,063,083	1981 S (proof only)			1995	.20
519,475,000	1982	.20		1995 D	.20
542,713,584	1982 D	.20		1995 S (proof only)	
3,857,479	1982 S (proof only)				
647,025,000	1983	.20			
730,129,224	1983 D	.20			
3,228,648	1983 S (proof only)				
856,669,000	1984	.20			
704,803,976	1984 D	.20			
3,065,110	1984 S (proof only)				
705,200,962	1985	.20			
587,979,970	1985 D	.20			
3,362,662	1985 S (proof only)				
682,649,693	1986	.20			

Twenty Cents

These silver coins were issued for a very short time, from 1875 to 1878. The difference between this coin and the popular quarter was too slight to make the twenty-cent piece useful. A peculiarity of this coin is that it had a smooth edge instead of the usual corrugated edge.

TWENTY CENT PIECES

The mint marks are under the eagle on the reverse.

QUANTITY	YEAR	GOOD TO VERY GOOD	FINE	VERY FINE	EXT. FINE	UNC.	PROOF
39,700	1875	$60.00	$80.00	$130.00	$215.00	$1000.00	$2500.00
1,155,000	1875 S	55.00	70.00	125.00	185.00	1000.00	
133,290	1875 CC	65.00	70.00	130.00	215.00	1100.00	
15,900	1876	80.00	115.00	165.00	250.00	1250.00	2500.00
10,000	1876 CC (extremely rare)						
510	1877 only proofs were struck						4000.00
600	1878 only proofs were struck						3750.00

Quarters

QUARTERS—DRAPED BUST TYPE

1796 1804–1807

QUANTITY	YEAR	ABOUT GOOD TO GOOD	VERY GOOD	FINE	VERY FINE
5,894	1796 rare	$1300.00	$2750.00	$5000.00	$10,500.00
6,738	1804	320.00	800.00	1800.00	4000.00
121,394	1805	135.00	200.00	300.00	900.00
206,124	1806 over 5	125.00	165.00	300.00	900.00
	1806	100.00	165.00	275.00	800.00
220,643	1807	100.00	165.00	275.00	800.00

QUARTERS—CAPPED BUST TYPE

QUANTITY	YEAR	ABOUT GOOD TO GOOD	VERY GOOD	FINE	VERY FINE	UNC.
69,232	1815	$40.00	$55.00	$85.00	$265.00	$3250.00
361,174	1818 over 15	45.00	55.00	85.00	275.00	2750.00
	1818	40.00	55.00	85.00	265.00	2250.00
144,000	1819	40.00	55.00	80.00	235.00	2000.00
127,444	1820	40.00	55.00	80.00	235.00	2000.00
216,851	1821	40.00	55.00	80.00	235.00	1800.00
64,080	1822	40.00	65.00	90.00	275.00	2500.00
	1822 25 over 50c (rare)	300.00	425.00	700.00	1250.00	8500.00

QUARTERS—CAPPED BUST TYPE (continued

QUANTITY	YEAR	ABOUT GOOD TO GOOD	VERY GOOD	FINE	VERY FINE	UNC.
17,000	1823 over 22					
	(extremely rare)	2000.00	5000.00	10,000.00	17,500.00	
?	1824	45.00	55.00	85.00	250.00	3200.00
168,000	1825 over 22	40.00	50.00	75.00	175.00	2600.00
	1825 over 23	40.00	50.00	75.00	175.00	2400.00
	1825 over 24	40.00	50.00	75.00	175.00	2700.00
4,000	1827 extremely rare, Superior August 1990 Sale, Proof					42,000.00
102,000	1828	40.00	50.00	65.00	200.00	2500.00
?	1828 25 over 50c	70.00	120.00	200.00	315.00	3200.00

QUANTITY	YEAR	GOOD TO VERY GOOD	FINE	VERY FINE	EXT. FINE	UNC.
398,000	1831	40.00	50.00	85.00	200.00	1100.00
320,000	1832	40.00	50.00	85.00	200.00	1100.00
156,000	1833	40.00	55.00	110.00	300.00	1200.00
286,000	1834	40.00	50.00	90.00	200.00	1100.00
1,952,000	1835	40.00	50.00	85.00	200.00	1100.00
472,000	1836	40.00	50.00	85.00	200.00	1100.00
252,400	1837	40.00	50.00	85.00	200.00	1200.00
832,000*	1838	40.00	50.00	85.00	200.00	1100.00

QUARTERS—LIBERTY SEATED TYPE

1838–1865   1866–1891

Without drapery from elbow
The mint marks are under the eagle on the reverse.

	* 1838	$13.50	$25.00	$50.00	$165.00	$1700.00
491,146	1839	13.50	22.50	45.00	160.00	1600.00
425,200	** 1840 O	13.50	22.50	45.00	150.00	1300.00

With drapery from elbow

188,127	1840	13.50	27.50	50.00	150.00	1200.00
	** 1840 O	12.50	25.00	45.00	160.00	1250.00
120,000	1841	25.00	45.00	70.00	175.00	900.00
452,000	1841 O	15.00	30.00	60.00	150.00	900.00
88,000	1842	37.50	85.00	130.00	250.00	1500.00
769,000	1842 O					
	large date	15.00	25.00	50.00	80.00	1100.00
	1842 O small date	50.00	200.00	400.00	800.00	3000.00

*Includes 1838 Liberty Seated quarters.
**Includes 1840 O quarters with drapery from elbow.

QUANTITY	YEAR	GOOD TO VERY GOOD	FINE	VERY FINE	EXT. FINE	UNC.
645,600	1843	15.00	25.00	35.00	75.00	700.00
968,000	1843 O	15.00	25.00	50.00	125.00	800.00
421,400	1844	15.00	25.00	35.00	75.00	700.00
740,000	1844 O	15.00	25.00	35.00	90.00	950.00
922,000	1845	15.00	25.00	35.00	75.00	700.00
510,000	1846	15.00	25.00	35.00	75.00	675.00
734,000	1847	15.00	25.00	35.00	75.00	675.00
368,000	1847 O	20.00	40.00	50.00	150.00	850.00
146,000	1848	20.00	40.00	70.00	200.00	1000.00
340,000	1849	20.00	40.00	50.00	125.00	900.00
?	1849 O	225.00	550.00	850.00	1500.00	4500.00
190,800	1850	15.00	35.00	70.00	120.00	900.00
412,000	1850 O	15.00	37.50	80.00	135.00	1000.00
160,000	1851	15.00	35.00	75.00	125.00	800.00
88,000	1851 O	125.00	350.00	550.00	1200.00	2750.00
177,060	1852	15.00	40.00	80.00	150.00	750.00
	Without drapery from elbow					
96,000	1852 O	200.00	350.00	550.00	1100.00	3250.00
?	1853 over 52 Rare					
	With arrows at date. Rays over eagle.					
15,254,220	1853	15.00	22.50	45.00	100.00	1100.00
1,332,000	1853 O	15.00	32.50	50.00	120.00	1300.00
	With arrows at date. Without rays.					
12,380,000	1854	12.00	17.50	35.00	75.00	800.00
1,484,000	1854 O	12.00	17.50	35.00	100.00	900.00
2,857,000	1855	12.00	17.50	35.00	75.00	850.00
176,000	1855 O	60.00	110.00	180.00	350.00	1600.00
396,400	1855 S	55.00	100.00	170.00	300.00	1500.00
	Without arrows at date					
7,264,000	1856	12.00	17.50	35.00	60.00	550.00
968,000	1856 O	12.00	17.50	35.00	75.00	850.00
286,000	1856 S	27.50	55.00	120.00	235.00	1200.00
9,644,000	1857	12.00	17.50	35.00	55.00	450.00
1,180,000	1857 O	12.00	17.50	35.00	60.00	800.00
82,000	1857 S	40.00	70.00	150.00	250.00	1600.00
7,368,000	1858	12.00	17.50	35.00	55.00	450.00
520,000	1858 O	12.00	17.50	35.00	55.00	850.00
121,000	1858 S	35.00	65.00	140.00	325.00	1500.00
1,344,000	1859	12.00	17.50	30.00	60.00	750.00
260,000	1859 O	12.00	17.50	40.00	85.00	1050.00
80,000	1859 S	60.00	150.00	275.00	475.00	2500.00
805,400	1860	12.00	17.50	30.00	50.00	500.00
388,000	1860 O	12.00	17.50	40.00	80.00	1000.00
56,000	1860 S	80.00	235.00	400.00	650.00	2500.00
4,854,600	1861	12.00	17.50	35.00	55.00	475.00
96,000	1861 S	40.00	75.00	150.00	250.00	2500.00
932,550	1862	12.00	17.50	30.00	55.00	500.00
67,000	1862 S	40.00	80.00	140.00	300.00	1900.00
192,060	1863	20.00	32.50	50.00	120.00	775.00
94,070	1864	35.00	60.00	150.00	200.00	1000.00
20,000	1864 S	130.00	300.00	450.00	900.00	3000.00
59,300	1865	45.00	80.00	115.00	225.00	900.00
41,000	1865 S	55.00	85.00	200.00	400.00	2500.00
	With motto over eagle					
17,525	1866	125.00	250.00	400.00	550.00	1300.00
28,005	1866 S	80.00	200.00	350.00	500.00	2000.00
20,620	1867	100.00	175.00	300.00	425.00	1200.00
48,000	1867 S	50.00	150.00	250.00	300.00	2000.00
30,000	1868	80.00	140.00	275.00	350.00	900.00
96,000	1868 S	65.00	110.00	180.00	240.00	1500.00
16,600	1869	150.00	340.00	400.00	550.00	1250.00
76,000	1869 S	65.00	150.00	250.00	300.00	1400.00
87,400	1870	40.00	80.00	140.00	225.00	850.00
8,340	1870 CC	725.00	2000.00	2750.00	5000.00	8000.00
171,232	1871	17.50	45.00	75.00	120.00	700.00
30,900	1871 S	125.00	325.00	550.00	825.00	2750.00
10,890	1871 CC	525.00	1000.00	2000.00	2750.00	8000.00

QUARTERS—LIBERTY SEATED TYPE (continued)

QUANTITY	YEAR	GOOD TO VERY GOOD	FINE	VERY FINE	EXT. FINE	UNC.
182,950	1872	15.00	45.00	70.00	125.00	550.00
83,000	1872 S	200.00	425.00	750.00	1100.00	4250.00
9,100	1872 CC	325.00	625.00	850.00	2500.00	6500.00
1,484,300*	1873 no arrows	15.00	30.00	75.00	150.00	800.00
16,462**	1873 CC no arrows	800.00	1000.00	2000.00	4250.00	
	With arrows at date					
*	1873	27.50	50.00	90.00	235.00	1000.00
156,000	1873 S	35.00	75.00	120.00	275.00	1250.00
**	1873 CC	725.00	1000.00	2250.00	4500.00	10,000.00
471,900	1874	22.50	40.00	75.00	185.00	1000.00
392,000	1874 S	30.00	50.00	90.00	215.00	1000.00
	Without arrows at date					
4,293,500	1875	10.00	15.00	25.00	50.00	375.00
680,000	1875 S	12.50	25.00	45.00	85.00	500.00
140,000	1875 CC	37.50	85.00	150.00	400.00	1500.00
17,817,150	1876	10.00	12.00	20.00	50.00	375.00
8,596,000	1876 S	9.00	12.00	20.00	50.00	400.00
4,944,000	1876 CC	10.00	20.00	35.00	75.00	450.00
10,911,710	1877	9.00	12.50	20.00	50.00	350.00
8,996,000	1877 S	9.00	12.50	20.00	50.00	375.00
4,192,000	1877 CC	10.00	15.00	25.00	80.00	500.00
2,260,800	1878	9.00	12.50	22.50	55.00	400.00
140,000	1878 S	60.00	70.00	125.00	225.00	1600.00
996,000	1878 CC	17.50	30.00	45.00	85.00	575.00
14,700	1879	70.00	150.00	175.00	225.00	650.00
14,955	1880	70.00	150.00	175.00	225.00	650.00
12,975	1881	75.00	160.00	185.00	265.00	700.00
16,300	1882	70.00	150.00	175.00	225.00	650.00
15,439	1883	70.00	150.00	175.00	225.00	650.00
8,875	1884	100.00	185.00	250.00	325.00	850.00
14,530	1885	70.00	150.00	175.00	225.00	750.00
5,886	1886	150.00	225.00	300.00	450.00	850.00
10,710	1887	125.00	175.00	225.00	350.00	700.00
10,833	1888	125.00	175.00	225.00	350.00	700.00
1,216,000	1888 S	10.00	12.50	22.50	50.00	400.00
12,711	1889	80.00	150.00	200.00	265.00	700.00
80,590	1890	45.00	70.00	90.00	150.00	600.00
3,920,600	1891	10.00	12.50	22.50	50.00	365.00
68,000	1891 O	125.00	220.00	375.00	500.00	2500.00
2,216,000	1891 S	10.00	16.00	27.50	55.00	375.00

*includes 1873 quarters with arrows.
**includes 1873 CC quarters with arrows.

QUARTERS—LIBERTY HEAD (BARBER) TYPE

The mint marks are under the eagle on the reverse.

QUANTITY	YEAR	GOOD	VERY GOOD	FINE	VERY FINE	EXT. FINE	UNC.	PROOF
8,237,245	1892	$3.00	$7.00	$10.00	$25.00	$55.00	$250.00	$850.00
2,640,000	1892 O	6.00	10.00	12.00	30.00	60.00	325.00	

QUANTITY	YEAR	GOOD	VERY GOOD	FINE	VERY FINE	EXT. FINE	UNC.	PROOF
964,079	1892 S	12.50	20.00	35.00	50.00	85.00	400.00	
5,444,815	1893	2.50	5.25	10.00	25.00	55.00	300.00	850.00
3,396,000	1893 O	3.00	7.50	12.50	30.00	65.00	320.00	
1,454,535	1893 S	7.00	11.00	16.00	37.50	70.00	350.00	
3,432,972	1894	2.50	5.50	10.00	25.00	55.00	300.00	850.00
2,852,000	1894 O	3.25	7.50	14.00	27.50	65.00	320.00	
2,648,821	1894 S	2.50	7.50	14.00	27.50	65.00	340.00	
4,440,880	1895	2.50	5.00	10.00	25.00	55.00	300.00	850.00
2,816,000	1895 O	3.00	7.150	14.00	27.50	65.00	400.00	
1,764,681	1895 S	6.00	10.00	16.00	32.50	65.00	340.00	
3,874,762	1896	2.50	5.00	10.00	25.00	55.00	300.00	850.00
1,484,000	1896 O	5.00	10.00	25.00	40.00	85.00	700.00	
188,039	1896 S	125.00	200.00	350.00	460.00	750.00	3000.00	
8,140,731	1897	2.50	4.00	10.00	22.50	55.00	300.00	850.00
1,414,800	1897 O	7.00	11.00	20.00	40.00	80.00	700.00	
542,229	1897 S	12.50	20.00	30.00	50.00	90.00	550.00	
11,100,735	1898	2.50	4.00	10.00	20.00	50.00	300.00	850.00
1,868,000	1898 O	3.50	7.00	15.00	30.00	60.00	425.00	
1,020,592	1898 S	6.00	10.00	16.00	30.00	55.00	475.00	
12,624,846	1899	2.50	4.00	10.00	22.50	50.00	300.00	850.00
2,644,000	1899 O	3.00	5.00	12.00	27.50	55.00	375.00	
708,000	1899 S	7.00	15.00	25.00	37.50	70.00	400.00	
10,016,912	1900	2.50	4.00	10.00	22.50	55.00	300.00	850.00
3,416,000	1900 O	5.00	11.00	15.00	25.00	60.00	350.00	
1,858,585	1900 S	2.50	5.00	12.50	22.50	50.00	350.00	
8,892,813	1901	2.50	4.00	10.00	22.50	45.00	300.00	850.00
1,612,000	1901 O	10.00	17.50	40.00	70.00	135.00	550.00	
72,664	1901 S	450.00	800.00	1000.00	1500.00	3500.00	10,000.00	
12,197,744	1902	2.50	4.00	9.00	22.50	55.00	300.00	850.00
4,748,000	1902 O	2.75	4.50	14.00	25.00	60.00	325.00	
1,524,612	1902 S	7.00	12.00	17.50	35.00	65.00	375.00	
9,670,064	1903	2.75	4.50	10.00	22.50	55.00	300.00	850.00
3,500,000	1903 O	2.75	5.00	12.50	35.00	70.00	375.00	
1,036,000	1903 S	7.00	12.00	25.00	55.00	70.00	425.00	
9,588,813	1904	2.75	4.50	10.00	22.50	55.00	300.00	850.00
2,456,000	1904 O	5.00	9.00	16.50	30.00	75.00	500.00	
4,968,250	1905	2.75	4.50	10.00	22.50	55.00	300.00	850.00
1,230,000	1905 O	5.50	12.00	20.00	40.00	65.00	375.00	
1,884,000	1905 S	4.00	6.50	12.50	27.50	60.00	325.00	
3,656,435	1906	2.75	5.00	10.00	22.50	60.00	300.00	850.00
3,280,000	1906 D	3.00	5.50	12.50	27.50	60.00	325.00	
2,056,000	1906 O	5.00	9.00	14.00	32.50	65.00	325.00	
7,192,575	1907	2.50	4.00	9.00	22.50	60.00	300.00	850.00
2,484,000	1907 D	3.50	6.50	12.50	27.50	60.00	325.00	
4,560,000	1907 O	2.75	6.50	12.00	25.00	55.00	325.00	
1,360,000	1907 S	3.50	6.50	12.50	27.50	65.00	325.00	
4,232,545	1908	2.50	4.50	10.00	22.50	55.00	300.00	850.00
5,788,000	1908 D	2.50	4.50	10.00	22.50	55.00	325.00	
6,244,000	1908 O	2.50	4.50	10.00	22.50	55.00	325.00	
784,000	1908 S	7.00	14.00	17.50	35.00	80.00	475.00	
9,268,650	1909	2.50	3.50	7.50	25.00	55.00	300.00	850.00
5,114,000	1909 D	2.50	3.50	7.50	25.00	55.00	325.00	
712,000	1909 O	10.00	17.50	35.00	70.00	125.00	600.00	
1,348,000	1909 S	2.75	4.25	9.00	24.00	55.00	350.00	
2,244,551	1910	2.50	3.50	9.00	24.00	55.00	300.00	850.00
1,500,000	1910 D	2.75	4.25	10.00	25.00	60.00	325.00	
3,720,543	1911	2.50	3.50	9.00	24.00	55.00	300.00	850.00
933,600	1911 D	3.50	5.50	17.50	35.00	70.00	325.00	
988,000	1911 S	3.50	4.25	12.50	25.00	65.00	340.00	
4,400,700	1912	2.50	3.50	9.00	24.00	55.00	300.00	850.00
708,000	1912 S	3.50	6.00	14.00	30.00	70.00	400.00	
484,613	1913	10.00	15.00	40.00	100.00	300.00	1200.00	900.00
1,450,800	1913 D	3.50	4.50	12.50	32.50	65.00	300.00	
40,000	1913 S	200.00	350.00	550.00	800.00	1500.00	3750.00	
6,244,610	1914	2.50	3.50	9.00	24.00	55.00	300.00	850.00
3,046,000	1914 D	2.50	3.50	9.00	24.00	55.00	300.00	
264,000	1914 S	12.50	15.00	30.00	60.00	200.00	625.00	

QUARTERS—LIBERTY HEAD (BARBER) TYPE (continued)

QUANTITY	YEAR	GOOD	VERY GOOD	FINE	VERY FINE	EXT. FINE	UNC.	PROOF
3,480,450	1915	2.50	3.50	9.00	24.00	55.00	300.00	1050.00
3,694,000	1915 D	2.50	3.50	9.00	24.00	55.00	325.00	
704,000	1915 S	3.00	5.00	12.50	27.50	60.00	375.00	
1,788,000	1916	2.50	3.50	9.00	24.00	55.00	300.00	
6,540,800	1916 D	2.50	3.50	9.00	24.00	55.00	325.00	

QUARTERS—STANDING LIBERTY TYPE

1916–1917   **1917–1930**

The mint marks are above and to the left of the date on the obverse.

QUANTITY	YEAR	GOOD	VERY GOOD	FINE	VERY FINE	EXT. FINE	UNC.
52,000	1916	$750.00	$1100.00	$1400.00	$1750.00	$2250.00	$5000.00
8,792,000	1917 type I*	7.50	10.00	15.00	25.00	55.00	225.00
1,509,200	1917 D type I*	7.50	11.00	17.50	27.50	60.00	250.00
1,952,000	1917 S type I*	7.50	11.00	17.50	27.50	60.00	250.00
13,880.00	1917 type II**	7.50	11.00	15.00	24.00	50.00	175.00
6,224,400	1719 D type II**	12.50	16.00	25.00	30.00	55.00	200.00
5,552,000	1917 S type II**	12.00	17.50	27.50	30.00	60.00	220.00
14,240,000	1819	7.00	10.00	14.00	20.00	40.00	165.00
7,380,000	1918 D	10.00	16.00	20.00	30.00	45.00	175.00
11,072,000	1819 S	7.00	10.00	15.00	22.50	40.00	140.00
?	1918 S (over 17)	500.00	625.00	1250.00	2000.00	3250.00	12,500.00
11,324,000	1919	10.00	15.00	20.00	30.00	40.00	150.00
1,944,000	1919 D	30.00	45.00	55.00	85.00	125.00	425.00
1,836,000	1919 S	30.00	50.00	55.00	80.00	150.00	400.00
27,860,000	1920	5.50	8.00	10.00	15.00	27.50	125.00
3,586,400	1920 D	12.50	20.00	30.00	42.00	70.00	200.00
6,380,000	1920 S	8.00	11.00	15.00	25.00	40.00	150.00
1,916,000	1921	40.00	65.00	115.00	140.00	200.00	400.00
9,716,000	1923	8.00	12.50	15.00	20.00	40.00	140.00
1,360,000	1923 S	60.00	90.00	125.00	200.00	300.00	500.00
10,920,000	1924	5.00	7.00	10.00	12.50	25.00	120.00
3,112,000	1924 D	16.00	24.00	30.00	40.00	50.00	130.00
2,860,000	1924 S	11.00	14.00	20.00	30.00	50.00	150.00
12,280,000	1925	3.00	4.00	4.50	9.00	25.00	100.00
11,316,000	1926	3.00	4.00	4.50	9.00	25.00	100.00
1,716,000	1926 D	3.25	4.00	7.00	14.00	35.00	115.00
2,700,000	1926 S	3.25	4.00	7.50	16.00	40.00	215.00
11,912,000	1927	3.00	4.00	4.50	9.00	25.00	100.00
976,400	1927 D	5.00	7.00	15.00	30.00	55.00	165.00
396,000	1927 S	10.00	15.00	50.00	150.00	625.00	4250.00
6,336,000	1928	3.00	4.00	4.50	9.00	22.50	100.00
1,627,600	1928 D	3.25	5.00	5.00	9.00	22.50	125.00
2,644,000	1928 S	3.00	4.00	4.75	9.00	22.50	120.00
11,140,000	1929	3.00	4.00	4.50	9.00	22.50	100.00
1,358,000	1929 D	3.25	4.50	6.00	9.00	25.00	120.00
1,764,000	1929 S	3.00	4.00	5.00	9.00	22.50	110.00
5,632,000	1930	3.00	4.00	5.00	9.00	22.50	100.00
1,556,000	1930 S	3.25	4.50	5.00	9.00	22.50	125.00

*stars at sides of eagle   **3 stars below eagle

QUARTERS—WASHINGTON TYPE

The mint marks are under the eagle on the reverse.

QUANTITY	YEAR	VERY GOOD	FINE	VERY FINE	EXT. FINE	UNC.
5,404,000	1932	$3.25	$3.75	$4.00	$5.00	$35.00
436,800	1932 D	45.00	55.00	65.00	125.00	500.00
408,000	1932 S	45.00	50.00	55.00	70.00	275.00
31,912,052	1934	2.75	3.25	3.50	5.00	30.00
3,527,200	1934 D	2.50	5.50	8.00	20.00	125.00
32,484,000	1935	2.50	3.25	3.50	4.00	18.00
5,780,000	1935 D	2.75	3.75	8.00	15.00	125.00
5,660,000	1935 S	2.75	3.75	7.00	11.00	70.00
41,303,837	1936	2.50	3.00	3.25	3.75	20.00
5,374,000	1936 D	2.75	6.50	15.00	40.00	250.00
3,828,000	1936 S	2.50	3.00	3.75	10.00	80.00
19,701,542	1937	2.50	3.00	3.25	4.00	30.00
7,189,600	1937 D	2.50	3.00	3.50	5.00	45.00
1,652,000	1937 S	6.50	8.50	11.00	22.50	110.00
9,480,045	1938	2.50	3.00	6.50	14.00	55.00
2,832,000	1938 S	2.75	5.00	6.50	11.00	65.00
33,548,795	1939	2.50	3.25	3.50	4.50	15.00
7,092,000	1939 D	2.75	3.50	3.75	4.75	32.50
2,628,000	1939 S	3.00	3.50	4.50	11.00	55.00
35,715,246	1940	2.50	3.00	3.25	4.50	16.00
2,797,600	1940 D	2.75	3.75	6.50	14.00	80.00
8,244,000	1940 S	2.75	3.25	4.00	4.50	20.00
79,047,287	1941	2.50	3.00	3.75	4.00	7.50
16,714,800	1941 D	2.50	3.00	3.75	4.50	25.00
16,080,000	1941 S	2.50	3.00	3.75	4.50	20.00

QUANTITY	YEAR	VERY FINE	EXT. FINE	MS-63
102,117,123	1942	2.50	4.00	10.00
17,487,200	1942 D	2.75	5.00	24.00
19,384,000	1942 S	3.75	7.00	65.00
99,700,000	1943	2.50	4.00	8.50
16,095,600	1943 D	3.00	5.00	40.00
21,700,000	1943 S	3.00	5.00	45.00
104,956,000	1944	2.50	3.75	6.00
14,600,000	1944 D	2.50	3.75	12.00
12,560,000	1944 S	3.00	4.00	13.50
74,372,000	1945	2.50	3.75	8.00
12,341,600	1945 D	2.50	3.75	11.00
17,004,001	1945 S	2.50	3.75	10.00
53,436,000	1946	2.50	3.75	6.00
9,072,800	1946 D	2.50	3.75	12.50
4,204,000	1946 S	3.00	4.25	10.00
22,556,000	1947	2.50	3.75	7.00
15,338,400	1947 D	2.50	3.75	7.00
5,532,000	1947 S	2.75	4.25	9.00
35,196,000	1948	2.50	3.75	7.00
16,766,800	1948 D	2.50	3.75	7.50
15,960,000	1948 S	2.50	3.75	7.00
9,312,000	1949	5.00	5.00	25.00
10,068,400	1949 D	3.00	4.50	12.50
24,971,512	1950	2.50	3.75	5.50
21,075,600	1950 D	2.50	3.75	6.00
10,284,600	1950 S	2.50	3.75	10.00
43,505,602	1951	2.50	3.75	5.50
35,354,800	1951 D	2.50	3.75	7.00
8,948,000	1951 S	3.00	3.00	12.50

QUARTERS—WASHINGTON TYPE (continued)

QUANTITY	YEAR	VERY GOOD	FINE	VERY FINE	EXT. FINE	UNC.
38,862,073	1952			2.50	4.25	5.50
49,795,200	1952 D			2.50	3.75	5.00
13,707,800	1952 S			2.50	3.75	9.00
18,664,920	1953			2.50	3.75	5.50
56,112,400	1953 D			2.50	3.75	5.00
14,016,000	1953 S			2.50	2.50	7.00
54,645,503	1954			2.50	2.50	5.00
46,305,000	1954 D			2.50	2.50	5.00
11,834,722	1954 S			2.50	2.50	5.00
18,558,381	1955			2.50	3.00	5.50
3,182,400	1955 D			3.00	2.50	7.00
44,325,081	1956				2.50	3.50
32,334,500	1956 D				2.50	3.50
46,720,000	1957				2.50	3.50
77,924,160	1957 D				2.50	3.50
6,360,000	1958				2.50	5.00
78,124,900	1958 D				2.50	3.50
24,374,000	1959				2.50	3.50
62,054,232	1959 D				2.50	3.50
29,164,000	1960				2.50	3.50
63,000,324	1960 D				2.50	3.50
40,064,244	1961				2.50	3.50
83,656,928	1961 D				2.50	3.50
39,374,019	1962				.50	3.50
127,554,756	1962 D				.50	3.50
77,391,645	1963				.50	3.50
135,288,184	1963 D				.50	3.50
570,390,585	1964				.50	3.50
704,135,528	1964 D				.50	3.50

QUANTITY	YEAR	UNC.	QUANTITY	YEAR	UNC.
1,817,357,540	1965	.75	215,048,000	1972	.60
818,836,911	1966	.75	311,067,732	1972 D	
1,524,031,848	1967	.75	3,267,667	1972 S (proof only)	.60
220,731,500	1968	.75	346,924,000	1973	.60
101,534,500	1968 D	.90	232,977,400	1973 D	
3,041,509	1968 S (proof only)		2,796,624	1973 S (proof only)	
176,212,000	1969	.60	*	1974	.60
114,372,000	1969 D	.75	*	1974 D	.60
2,934,631	1969 S (proof only)		2,617,350	1974 S (proof only)	
136,420,000	1970	.60	809,784,016	1976 Copper-nickel clad	1.00
417,341,364	1970 D	.60	860,118,839	1976 D Copper-nickel clad	1.00
2,632,810	1970 S (proof only)		7,059,099	1976 S Copper-nickel clad (proof)	
109,284,000	1971	.60			
258,634,428	1971 D	.60	**11,000,000	1976 S Silver clad	5.00
3,224,138	1971 S (proof only)	.60	**4,000,000	1976 S Silver Clad (proof)	

*Mintage continued into 1975—struck simultaneously with Bicentennial coins dated 1776–1976.
**Approximate mintage. Not all released.

Bicentennial coins dated 1776–1976.

QUANTITY	YEAR	MS-63
468,556,000	1977	.50
256,524,978	1977 D	.50
3,251,152	1977 S (proof only)	
521,452,000	1978	.50
287,373,152	1978 D	.50
3,127,781	1978 S (proof only)	
515,708,000	1979	.50
489,789,780	1979 D	.50
3,677,175	1979 S (proof only)	
635,832,000	1980	.50
518,327,427	1980 D	.50
3,554,806	1980 S (proof only)	
601,716,000	1981	.50
575,722,833	1981 D	.50
4,063,083	1981 S (proof only)	
500,931,000	1982	.50
480,042,788	1982 D	.50
3,857,479	1982 S (proof only)	
673,535,000	1983	.50
617,806,446	1983 D	.50
3,228,648	1983 S (proof only)	
676,545,000	1984	.50
546,483,064	1984 D	.50
3,065,110	1984 S (proof only)	
775,818,962	1985	.50
519,962,888	1985 D	.50
3,362,662	1985 S (proof only)	
551,199,333	1986	.50
504,298,660	1986 D	.50
3,010,497	1986 S (proof only)	
582,499,481	1987	.50
655,594,696	1987 D	.50
3,792,233	1987 S (proof only)	
562,052,000	1988	.50

QUANTITY	YEAR	MS-63
	1988 S (proof only)	
596,810,688	1988 D	.50
512,868,000	1989	.50
896,535,597	1989 D	.50
3,220,194	1989 S (proof only)	
613,792,000	1990	.50
927,638,181	1990 D	.50
3,299,559	1990 S (proof only)	
570,968,000	1991	.50
630,966,693	1991 D	.50
2,867,787	1991 S (proof only)	
384,764,000	1992	.50
389,777,107	1992 D	.50
2,858,981	1992 S (proof only)	
639,276,000	1993	.50
645,476,128	1993 D	.50
2,633,439	1993 S (proof only)	
	1994	.50
	1994 D	.50
	1994 S (proof only)	
	1995	150
	1995 D	.50
	1995 S (proof only)	

Half Dollars

HALF DOLLARS—FLOWING HAIR TYPE

QUANTITY	YEAR	GOOD TO VERY GOOD	FINE	VERY FINE
23,464	1794	$1000.00	$2500.00	$3750.00
299,680	1795	550.00	750.00	1500.00

HALF DOLLARS—DRAPED BUST TYPE

1796–1797   **1801–1807**

QUANTITY	YEAR	GOOD TO VERY GOOD	FINE	VERY FINE
?	1796 15 stars, rare	$8500.00	$15,000.00	$25,000.00
?	1796 16 stars, rare	8500.00	15,000.00	25,000.00
3,918	1797 rare	8000.00	12,500.00	22,500.00
30,289	1801	200.00	500.00	850.00
29,890	1802	165.00	400.00	650.00
31,715	1803	125.00	250.00	550.00
156,519	1805 over 4	150.00	375.00	575.00
211,722	1805	80.00	200.00	400.00
839,576	1806 over 5	85.00	175.00	400.00
	1806 over 9 (inverted 6)	135.00	285.00	500.00
	1806	75.00	185.00	450.00
301,076	1807 bust right	75.00	150.00	400.00

HALF DOLLARS—CAPPED BUST TYPE

QUANTITY	YEAR	FINE	VERY FINE	EXT. FINE	UNC.
750,500	1807 bust left	$125.00	$275.00	$500.00	$2250.00
	1807 50 over 20	75.00	175.00	325.00	1750.00
1,368,600	1808 over 7	60.00	100.00	250.00	1100.00
	1808	37.50	70.00	175.00	1000.00
1,405,810	1809	35.00	65.00	175.00	900.00
1,276,276	1810	35.00	65.00	150.00	850.00
1,203,644	1811	35.00	65.00	160.00	900.00
	1811 as 18.11	65.00	135.00	160.00	1100.00
1,628,059	1812 over 11	60.00	100.00	175.00	1100.00
	1812	40.00	65.00	160.00	1000.00
1,241,903	1813	40.00	65.00	150.00	950.00

QUANTITY	YEAR	FINE	VERY FINE	EXT. FINE	UNC.
1,039,075	1814 over 13	50.00	80.00	200.00	1000.00
	1814	40.00	65.00	175.00	850.00
47,015	1815 over 12	650.00	1100.00	1650.00	6500.00
1,215,567	1817 over 13	65.00	175.00	500.00	1500.00
	1817	40.00	70.00	150.00	850.00
	1817 as 181.7	50.00	85.00	200.00	950.00
1,960,322	1818	40.00	75.00	125.00	800.00
	1818 over 17	40.00	75.00	125.00	900.00
2,208,000	1819 over 18	40.00	80.00	100.00	900.00
	1819	35.00	75.00	85.00	850.00
751,122	1820 over 19	50.00	90.00	175.00	900.00
	1820	50.00	100.00	185.00	1000.00
1,305,797	1821	40.00	70.00	120.00	800.00
1,559,573	1822	40.00	70.00	120.00	800.00
	1822 over 21	100.00	175.00	300.00	1250.00
1,694,200	1823 over 22	100.00	150.00	150.00	1000.00
	1823	35.00	70.00	120.00	800.00
3,504,954	1824 over other dates	35.00	70.00	100.00	850.00
	1824 over 21	35.00	65.00	100.00	800.00
	1824	35.00	65.00	90.00	700.00
2,934,166	1825	35.00	65.00	90.00	700.00
4,004,180	1826	35.00	65.00	90.00	700.00
5,493,400	1827 over 26	32.50	50.00	80.00	700.00
	1827	32.50	50.00	75.00	700.00
3,075,200	1828	32.50	45.00	70.00	650.00
3,712,156	1829 over 27	32.50	55.00	75.00	700.00
	1829	30.00	45.00	70.00	650.00
4,764,800	1830	27.50	45.00	70.00	650.00
5,873,660	1831	27.50	45.00	70.00	650.00
4,797,000	1832	27.50	45.00	70.00	650.00
5,206,000	1833	27.50	45.00	70.00	650.00
6,412,004	1834	27.50	45.00	70.00	650.00
5,352,006	1835	27.50	45.00	70.00	650.00
6,546,200	1836 lettered edge	27.50	45.00	70.00	650.00
	1836 milled edge	500.00	1100.00	2000.00	6500.00
3,629,820	1837	55.00	100.00	200.00	1000.00
3,546,000	1838	55.00	100.00	200.00	1000.00
20	1838 O (extremely rare)				50,000.00
3,334,560	*1839	55.00	100.00	200.00	1000.00
162,976	1839 O mint mark on obv.	200.00	325.00	500.00	3750.00

*includes 1839 Liberty Seated half dollars

HALF DOLLARS—LIBERTY SEATED TYPE

1839–1865   1866–1891

The mint marks are under the eagle on the reverse.

HALF DOLLARS—LIBERTY SEATED TYPE (continued)

QUANTITY (see above)	YEAR	GOOD TO VERY GOOD	FINE	VERY FINE	EXT. FINE	UNC.
	1839 no drapery	$45.00	$80.00	$150.00	$350.00	$5000.00
	1839 with drapery	20.00	30.00	50.00	80.00	500.00
1,435,008	1840 small letters	15.00	25.00	40.00	75.00	500.00
	1840 large letters	40.00	70.00	120.00	200.00	550.00
855,100	1840 O	20.00	25.00	50.00	85.00	600.00
310,000	1841	20.00	40.00	65.00	125.00	650.00
401,000	1841 O	20.00	40.00	50.00	85.00	650.00
2,012,764	1842	20.00	35.00	45.00	80.00	600.00
?	1842 O small date (rare)	200.00	500.00	1000.00	3500.00	Rare
957,000	1842 O large date	20.00	35.00	50.00	85.00	600.00
3,844,000	1843	20.00	35.00	45.00	80.00	575.00
2,268,000	1843 O	20.00	35.00	45.00	80.00	550.00
1,766,000	1844	20.00	35.00	45.00	80.00	550.00
2,005,000	1844 O	17.50	30.00	40.00	80.00	550.00
589,000	1845	20.00	35.00	45.00	90.00	600.00
2,094,000	1845 O	17.50	30.00	45.00	85.00	550.00
2,210,000	1846 horizontal 6 error	65.00	120.00	165.00	300.00	1000.00
	1846	17.50	30.00	45.00	85.00	550.00
2,304,000	1846 O small date	17.50	30.00	45.00	85.00	550.00
	1846 O large date	45.00	125.00	300.00	425.00	1300.00
1,156,000	1847 over 46	500.00	1000.00	1750.00	5000.00	Rare
	1847	17.50	30.00	45.00	85.00	575.00
2,584,000	1847 O	17.50	30.00	45.00	85.00	575.00
580,000	1848	17.50	30.00	45.00	85.00	575.00
3,180,000	1848 O	17.50	30.00	45.00	85.00	575.00
1,252,000	1849	17.50	30.00	45.00	85.00	575.00
2,310,000	1849 O	17.50	30.00	45.00	85.00	575.00
227,000	1850	45.00	85.00	135.00	250.00	850.00
2,456,000	1850 O	17.50	30.00	45.00	90.00	600.00
200,750	1851	35.00	85.00	125.00	250.00	850.00
402,000	1851 O	25.00	50.00	75.00	125.00	600.00
77,130	1852	75.00	225.00	400.00	625.00	1350.00
144,000	1852 O	40.00	75.00	125.00	250.00	1100.00
?	1853 no arrows (extremely rare)					
3,532,708	1853 arrows	20.00	45.00	90.00	250.00	2250.00
1,328,000	1853 O arrows	20.00	45.00	90.00	250.00	2250.00
2,982,000	1854	15.00	30.00	50.00	80.00	750.00
5,240,000	1854 O	15.00	25.00	40.00	75.00	750.00
759,500	1855	15.00	30.00	50.00	100.00	750.00
3,688,000	1855 O	15.00	25.00	40.00	90.00	750.00
129,950	1855 S rare	175.00	350.00	625.00	1250.00	6250.00
938,000	1856	16.00	30.00	50.00	75.00	550.00
2,658,000	1856 O	15.00	30.00	50.00	75.00	550.00
211,000	1856 S	25.00	40.00	100.00	200.00	1000.00
1,988,000	1857	15.00	30.00	50.00	85.00	550.00
818,000	1857 O	16.00	35.00	50.00	85.00	550.00
158,000	1857 S	30.00	50.00	100.00	200.00	1250.00
4,226,000	1858	15.00	25.00	40.00	70.00	500.00
7,294,000	1858 O	15.00	25.00	40.00	70.00	500.00
476,000	1858 S	20.00	35.00	50.00	100.00	750.00
748,000	1859	15.00	25.00	40.00	70.00	500.00
2,834,000	1859 O	14.00	25.00	40.00	70.00	500.00
566,000	1859 S	17.50	35.00	55.00	120.00	800.00
303,700	1860	15.00	25.00	40.00	85.00	750.00
1,290,000	1860 O	15.00	25.00	40.00	75.00	625.00
472,000	1860 S	17.50	30.00	50.00	85.00	650.00
2,888,400	1861	15.00	25.00	40.00	75.00	500.00
2,532,633	*1861 O	15.00	25.00	40.00	75.00	500.00
939,500	1861 S	15.00	25.00	40.00	75.00	550.00
252,350	1862	20.00	35.00	80.00	175.00	825.00
1,352,000	1862 S	17.50	30.00	45.00	90.00	750.00
503,660	1863	17.50	30.00	45.00	90.00	750.00

QUANTITY	YEAR	GOOD TO VERY GOOD	FINE	VERY FINE	EXT. FINE	UNC.
916,000	1863 S	17.50	30.00	45.00	90.00	750.00
379,570	1864	17.50	30.00	45.00	90.00	750.00
658,000	1864 S	17.50	30.00	45.00	90.00	800.00
511,900	1865	17.50	30.00	45.00	100.00	875.00
675,000	1865 S	17.50	30.00	45.00	90.00	800.00
745,625	1866 motto	15.00	25.00	35.00	70.00	800.00
1,054,000	1866 S no motto	65.00	135.00	275.00	450.00	4250.00
	1866 S motto	15.00	25.00	37.50	75.00	525.00
424,325	1867	15.00	25.00	37.50	75.00	525.00
1,196,000	1867 S	15.00	25.00	37.50	75.00	525.00
378,200	1868	15.00	25.00	37.50	75.00	525.00
1,160,000	1868 S	15.00	25.00	37.50	75.00	525.00
795,900	1869	15.00	25.00	37.50	75.00	525.00
656,000	1869 S	15.00	25.00	37.50	75.00	525.00
600,900	1870	15.00	25.00	37.50	75.00	525.00
1,004,000	1870 S	15.00	25.00	37.50	75.00	525.00
54,617	1870 CC	325.00	1100.00	1500.00	3750.00	7500.00
1,165,350	1871	15.00	25.00	37.50	50.00	525.00
2,178,000	1871 S	15.00	25.00	37.50	65.00	575.00
139,950	1871 CC	100.00	200.00	400.00	750.00	4750.00
881,550	1872	15.00	25.00	40.00	75.00	525.00
580,000	1872 S	15.00	25.00	40.00	75.00	550.00
272,000	1872 CC	65.00	125.00	250.00	425.00	2250.00
2,617,500	1873 no arrows	15.00	25.00	40.00	75.00	525.00
	1873 arrows	30.00	65.00	125.00	200.00	875.00
337,060	1873 CC no arrows	75.00	150.00	250.00	500.00	2500.00
	1873 CC arrows	70.00	125.00	225.00	350.00	2250.00
233,000	1873 S	35.00	65.00	125.00	250.00	1100.00
2,360,300	1874	27.50	55.00	115.00	225.00	1100.00
394,000	1874 S	40.00	85.00	135.00	275.00	1500.00
59,000	1874 CC	125.00	275.00	525.00	1000.00	4750.00
6,027,500	1875	15.00	25.00	37.50	75.00	475.00
3,200,000	1875 S	15.00	25.00	37.50	75.00	500.00
1,008,000	1875 CC	17.50	30.00	50.00	85.00	575.00
8,419,150	1876	15.00	25.00	37.50	70.00	500.00
4,528,000	1876 S	15.00	25.00	37.50	70.00	475.00
1,956,000	1876 CC	17.50	35.00	50.00	110.00	650.00
8,304,510	1877	15.00	25.00	37.50	70.00	550.00
5,356,000	1877 S	15.00	25.00	37.50	70.00	575.00
1,420,000	1877 CC	17.50	35.00	55.00	100.00	600.00
1,378,400	1878	15.00	25.00	40.00	70.00	500.00
12,000	1878 S	2000.00	3500.00	5000.00	10,000.00	27,500.00
62,000	1878 CC	175.00	300.00	650.00	1250.00	3750.00
5,900	1879	125.00	175.00	275.00	350.00	1000.00
9,755	1880	100.00	150.00	200.00	275.00	825.00
10,975	1881	100.00	150.00	200.00	275.00	825.00
5,500	1882	125.00	200.00	250.00	375.00	900.00
9,039	1883	100.00	150.00	200.00	275.00	825.00
5,275	1884	125.00	200.00	275.00	350.00	900.00
6,130	1885	125.00	200.00	275.00	350.00	900.00
5,886	1886	135.00	175.00	275.00	400.00	900.00
5,710	1887	125.00	200.00	275.00	400.00	900.00
12,833	1888	100.00	150.00	200.00	275.00	850.00
12,711	1889	100.00	150.00	200.00	275.00	850.00
12,590	1890	100.00	150.00	200.00	275.00	850.00
200,600	1891	20.00	35.00	75.00	85.00	600.00

*All but 300,000 of these coins were struck after the Confederate forces seized the New Orleans Mint.

HALF DOLLARS—LIBERTY HEAD (BARBER) TYPE

The mint marks are to the left of "half dollar" on the reverse.

QUANTITY	YEAR	GOOD	VERY GOOD	FINE	VERY FINE	EXT. FINE	UNC.	PROOF
935,245	1892	$8.00	$12.50	$30.00	$50.00	$130.00	$500.00	$1100.00
390,000	1892 O	80.00	90.00	130.00	230.00	325.00	850.00	
1,029,028	1892 S	60.00	85.00	125.00	200.00	300.00	900.00	
1,826,792	1893	8.00	12.50	30.00	50.00	130.00	580.00	1000.00
1,389,000	1893 O	17.50	25.00	40.00	75.00	130.00	700.00	
740,000	1893 S	45.00	65.00	90.00	135.00	200.00	825.00	
1,148,972	1894	8.00	15.00	27.50	45.00	130.00	625.00	1000.00
2,138,000	1894 O	8.00	15.00	30.00	50.00	140.00	700.00	
4,048,690	1894 S	6.00	9.00	25.00	42.50	125.00	650.00	
1,835,218	1895	6.00	9.00	27.50	42.50	125.00	600.00	1000.00
1,766,000	1895 O	9.00	12.50	35.00	45.00	135.00	650.00	
1,108,086	1895 S	15.00	25.00	27.50	60.00	135.00	650.00	
950,762	1896	7.00	12.00	35.00	45.00	135.00	650.00	1000.00
924,000	1896 O	15.00	20.00	35.00	65.00	175.00	800.00	
1,140,948	1896 S	37.50	50.00	75.00	120.00	225.00	850.00	
2,480,731	1897	6.50	9.00	17.50	40.00	160.00	700.00	1000.00
632,000	1897 O	40.00	55.00	75.00	125.00	225.00	900.00	
933,900	1897 S	40.00	60.00	80.00	135.00	250.00	900.00	
2,956,735	1898	6.50	9.00	15.00	40.00	125.00	600.00	1000.00
874,000	1898 O	12.00	17.50	35.00	50.00	160.00	700.00	
2,358,550	1898 S	7.50	11.00	20.00	50.00	130.00	650.00	
5,538,846	1899	5.50	7.50	15.00	37.50	120.00	550.00	1000.00
1,724,000	1899 O	6.00	8.50	20.00	50.00	120.00	575.00	
1,686,411	1899 S	9.00	12.50	25.00	50.00	120.00	600.00	
4,762,912	1900	6.25	7.00	12.00	37.50	120.00	550.00	1000.00
2,744,000	1900 O	6.25	7.50	12.50	40.00	130.00	600.00	
2,560,322	1900 S	7.00	10.00	12.50	40.00	125.00	600.00	
4,268,813	1901	6.25	7.50	12.00	37.50	115.00	500.00	1000.00
1,124,000	1901 O	6.00	10.00	20.00	55.00	200.00	900.00	
847,044	1901 S	11.00	20.00	50.00	125.00	250.00	1200.00	
4,922,777	1902	6.25	7.50	12.50	37.50	115.00	525.00	1000.00
2,526,000	1902 O	6.25	7.50	12.50	37.50	115.00	650.00	
1,460,670	1902 S	6.25	8.00	15.00	40.00	115.00	600.00	
2,278,755	1903	6.25	7.50	25.00	37.50	115.00	550.00	1000.00
2,100,000	1903 O	6.25	7.50	17.50	37.50	115.00	650.00	
1,920,772	1903 S	5.00	8.00	20.00	40.00	115.00	650.00	
2,992,670	1904	5.50	7.00	12.50	37.50	115.00	500.00	1000.00
1,117,600	1904 O	6.25	9.00	15.00	40.00	140.00	850.00	
553,038	1904 S	11.00	20.00	37.50	80.00	200.00	900.00	
662,727	1905	6.25	11.00	25.00	55.00	150.00	650.00	1000.00
505,000	1905 O	10.00	17.50	35.00	70.00	175.00	650.00	
2,494,000	1905 S	5.50	6.50	12.50	37.50	125.00	600.00	
2,638,675	1906	6.25	7.00	12.50	37.50	125.00	550.00	1000.00
4,028,000	1906 D	6.25	7.00	12.50	37.50	115.00	525.00	
2,446,000	1906 O	6.25	7.00	12.50	37.50	115.00	550.00	
1,740,154	1906 S	6.50	7.50	13.50	40.00	120.00	600.00	
2,598,575	1907	6.25	7.00	12.50	37.50	115.00	575.00	1000.00
3,856,000	1907 D	6.25	7.00	12.50	37.50	115.00	575.00	
3,946,600	1907 O	6.25	7.00	12.50	37.50	115.00	600.00	
1,250,000	1907 S	6.25	7.00	13.50	37.50	115.00	600.00	

QUANTITY	YEAR	GOOD	VERY GOOD	FINE	VERY FINE	EXT. FINE	UNC.	PROOF
1,354,545	1908	6.25	7.00	13.50	37.50	115.00	575.00	1000.00
3,280,000	1908 D	6.25	7.00	12.50	37.50	115.00	575.00	
5,360,000	1908 O	6.25	7.00	12.50	37.50	115.00	600.00	
1,644,828	1908 S	6.25	7.00	13.50	37.50	115.00	625.00	
2,368,650	1909	6.25	7.00	12.50	37.50	115.00	550.00	1000.00
925,400	1909 O	6.25	7.00	13.50	37.50	115.00	750.00	
1,764,000	1909 S	6.25	7.00	12.50	37.50	115.00	600.00	
418,551	1910	7.00	12.50	22.50	50.00	135.00	700.00	1100.00
1,948,000	1910 S	6.25	7.00	12.50	37.50	115.00	575.00	
1,406,543	1911	6.25	7.00	12.50	37.50	115.00	575.00	1000.00
695,080	1911 D	6.25	7.00	14.00	40.00	115.00	575.00	
1,272,000	1911 S	6.25	7.00	12.50	37.50	115.00	550.00	
1,550,700	1912	6.25	7.00	12.50	37.50	115.00	550.00	1000.00
2,300,800	1912 D	6.25	7.00	12.50	37.50	115.00	550.00	
1,370,000	1912 S	6.25	7.00	12.50	37.50	115.00	600.00	
188,627	1913	15.00	20.00	37.50	70.00	150.00	750.00	1200.00
534,000	1913 D	6.25	8.00	12.50	45.00	115.00	575.00	
604,000	1913 S	6.25	7.50	14.00	40.00	125.00	625.00	
124,610	1914	25.00	30.00	50.00	90.00	190.00	800.00	1400.00
992,000	1914 S	6.25	7.00	12.50	40.00	115.00	600.00	
138,450	1915	18.00	25.00	45.00	80.00	150.00	875.00	1200.00
1,170,400	1915 D	6.25	7.00	12.50	37.50	115.00	550.00	
1,604,000	1915 S	6.25	7.00	12.50	37.50	115.00	550.00	

HALF DOLLARS—WALKING LIBERTY TYPE

The mint marks are to the left of "half dollar" on the reverse.

QUANTITY	YEAR	GOOD	VERY GOOD	FINE	VERY FINE	EXT. FINE	UNC.
608,000	1916	$15.00	$24.00	$40.00	$75.00	$150.00	$325.00
1,014,400	1916 D on obv	10.00	15.00	27.50	55.00	120.00	300.00
508,000	1916 S on obv	35.00	40.00	90.00	200.00	300.00	725.00
12,992,000	1917	6.50	7.50	9.00	12.50	30.00	150.00
765,400	1917 D on obv	7.00	12.00	35.00	60.00	120.00	450.00
1,940,000	1917 D on rev	6.50	8.50	20.00	40.00	100.00	525.00
952,000	1917 S on obv	8.00	15.00	40.00	100.00	225.00	1000.00
5,554,000	1917 S on rev	6.50	8.00	10.00	20.00	40.00	300.00
6,634,000	1918	6.50	7.50	7.50	20.00	100.00	325.00
3,853,040	1918 D	6.50	8.00	8.50	35.00	100.00	650.00
10,282,000	1918 S	6.50	7.50	7.50	17.50	70.00	325.00
962,000	1919	7.00	9.00	20.00	85.00	200.00	1000.00
1,165,000	1919 D	7.00	9.00	20.00	100.00	275.00	1650.00
1,552,000	1919 S	6.50	7.50	18.00	75.00	240.00	1800.00
6,372,000	1920	6.50	7.00	10.00	17.50	45.00	250.00
1,551,000	1920 D	6.50	7.50	12.50	70.00	150.00	1000.00
4,624,000	1920 S	6.50	7.50	12.00	35.00	90.00	900.00
246,000	1921	40.00	55.00	90.00	220.00	650.00	1900.00
208,000	1921 D	65.00	80.00	125.00	225.00	750.00	2100.00
548,000	1921 S	12.00	17.50	37.50	200.00	650.00	6500.00
2,178,000	1923 S	6.50	7.00	9.00	40.00	110.00	900.00
2,392,000	1927 S	6.50	7.00	9.00	25.00	65.00	650.00
1,940,000	1928 S		6.50	7.00	25.00	90.00	750.00

HALF DOLLARS—WALKING LIBERTY TYPE (continued)

QUANTITY	YEAR	GOOD	VERY GOOD	FINE	VERY FINE	EXT. FINE	UNC.
1,001,200	1929 D		7.00	8.00	20.00	45.00	350.00
1,902,000	1929 S		6.50	7.00	12.50	40.00	350.00
1,786,000	1933 S		6.50	7.00	17.50	50.00	400.00
6,964,000	1934		6.50	7.00	9.00	11.00	65.00
2,361,400	1934 D		6.50	7.50	10.00	30.00	225.00
3,652,000	1934 S		6.50	7.00	8.00	25.00	300.00
9,162,000	1935		6.50	7.00	8.00	10.00	60.00
3,003,800	1935 D		6.50	7.00	7.50	25.00	210.00
3,854,000	1935 S		6.50	7.00	7.50	30.00	250.00
12,617,901	1936		6.50	7.00	7.50	10.00	55.00
4,252,400	1936 D		6.50	7.00	8.00	15.00	120.00
3,884,000	1936 S		6.50	7.00	8.00	20.00	175.00
9,527,728	1937		6.50	7.00	7.50	9.00	55.00
1,760,001	1937 D		6.50	7.00	8.00	27.50	225.00
2,090,000	1937 S		6.50	7.00	7.50	20.00	175.00
4,118,152	1938		6.50	7.50	8.00	12.50	90.00
491,600	1938 D		27.50	30.00	37.50	75.00	450.00
6,820,808	1939		6.50	7.00	7.50	9.00	65.00
4,267,800	1939 D		6.50	7.00	7.50	10.00	65.00
2,552,000	1939 S		6.50	7.00	7.50	15.00	100.00
9,167,279	1940				6.50	9.00	55.00
4,550,000	1940 S				6.50	12.00	85.00
24,207,412	1941				6.50	8.00	50.00
11,248,400	1941 D				6.50	8.50	60.00
8,098,000	1941 S				8.00	15.00	175.00
47,839,120	1942				6.50	8.00	50.00
10,973,800	1942 D				7.50	10.00	65.00
12,708,000	1942 S				7.50	12.50	110.00
53,190,000	1943				6.50	8.00	55.00
11,346,000	1943 D				6.50	9.00	60.00
13,450,000	1943 S				6.50	8.50	55.00
28,206,000	1944				6.50	7.50	45.00
9,769,000	1944 D				6.50	9.00	65.00
8,904,000	1944 S				6.50	9.00	70.00
31,502,000	1945				6.50	8.00	50.00
9,966,800	1945 D				6.50	9.00	65.00
10,156,000	1945 S				6.50	9.00	70.00
12,118,000	1946				6.50	9.00	55.00
2,151,100	1946 D				6.50	9.00	65.00
3,724,000	1946 S				6.50	9.00	75.00
4,094,000	1947				6.50	10.00	70.00
3,900,000	1947 D				6.50	10.00	70.00

HALF DOLLARS—FRANKLIN TYPE

The mint marks are above the Liberty Bell on the reverse.

QUANTITY	YEAR	VERY FINE	EXT. FINE	UNC.
3,006,814	1948	$6.50	$7.50	$20.00
4,028,600	1948 D	6.50	7.50	17.50
5,714,000	1949	6.50	8.00	45.00
4,120,600	1949 D	6.50	8.00	40.00
3,744,000	1949 S	7.00	11.00	70.00
7,793,509	1950	6.50	7.50	40.00
8,031,600	1950 D	6.50	7.50	30.00
16,859,602	1951	6.50	7.50	17.50
9,475,200	1951 D	6.50	7.50	30.00
13,696,000	1951 S	6.50	7.50	22.00
21,274,073	1952	6.50	7.50	15.00
25,395,600	1952 D	6.50	7.50	11.00
5,526,000	1952 S	6.50	7.50	30.00
2,796,920	1953	6.50	8.00	22.50
20,900,400	1953 D	6.50	7.50	14.00
4,148,000	1953 S	6.50	7.50	25.00
13,421,503	1954	6.50	7.50	12.50
25,445,580	1954 D	6.50	7.50	12.00
4,993,400	1954 S	6.50	7.50	15.00
2,876,381	1955	6.50	9.00	18.50

QUANTITY	YEAR	EXT. FINE	UNC.	QUANTITY	YEAR	EXT. FINE	UNC.
4,213,081	1956	$6.50	$12.50	18,215,812	1960 D	$6.50	$8.50
5,150,000	1957	6.50	12.50	11,318,244	1961	6.50	8.50
19,966,850	1957 D	6.50	10.00	20,276,442	1961 D	6.50	7.50
4,042,000	1958	6.50	12.00	12,932,019	1962	6.50	7.50
23,962,412	1958 D	6.50	10.00	70,473,281	1962 D	6.50	7.50
6,200,000	1959	6.50	10.00	77,391,645	1963	6.50	7.50
13,053,750	1959 D	6.50	10.00	135,288,184	1963 D	6.50	7.50
6,024,000	1960	6.50	10.00				

HALF DOLLARS—KENNEDY TYPE

The mint marks are near the claw holding the laurel wreath on the reverse.

QUANTITY	YEAR	MS-65	QUANTITY	YEAR	MS-65
273,304,004	1964	$7.50	302,097,424	1971 D	2.00
156,205,446	1964 D	7.50	3,267,667	1971 S (proof only)	
63,519,366	1965	4.00	153,180,000	1972	2.00
106,723,349	1966	3.75	141,890,000	1972 D	2.00
295,046,978	1967	3.75	3,267,667	1972 S (proof only)	
246,951,930	1968 D	3.75	64,964,000	1973	2.00
3,041,509	1968 S (proof only)		83,171,400	1973 D	2.00
129,881,800	1969 D	3.75	2,769,624	1973 S (proof only)	
2,934,631	1969 S (proof only)		*	1974	2.00
2,150,000	1970 D	30.00	*	1974 D	2.00
2,632,810	1970 S (proof only)		2,617,350	1974 S (proof only)	
155,164,000	1971	2.00			

*Mintage continued into 1975—struck simultaneously with Bicentennial coins dated 1776–1976.

Mintage of Bicentennial coins dated 1776–1976 began in March 1975.

QUANTITY	YEAR	MS-65
234,308,000	1976 Copper-nickel clad	1.50
287,565,248	1976 D Copper-nickel clad	1.50
	1976 S Copper-nickel clad (proof)	
*4,239,722	1976 S Silver clad	10.00
	1976 S Silver clad (proof)	

*Approximate mintage. Not all released.

QUANTITY	YEAR	MS-65	QUANTITY	YEAR	MS-65
43,598,000	1977	1.00		1987	1.00
31,449,106	1977 D	1.00		1987 D	1.00
3,251,152	1977 S (proof only)		3,792,233	1987 S (proof only)	
14,350,000	1978	1.00	13,626,000	1988	1.00
13,765,799	1978 D	1.00	12,000,096	1988 D	1.00
3,127,781	1978 S (proof only)		3,262,948	1988 S (proof only)	
68,312,000	1979	1.00	24,542,000	1989	1.00
15,815,422	1979 D	1.00	23,000,216	1989 D	1.00
3,677,175	1979 S (proof only)		3,215,728	1989 S (proof only)	
44,134,000	1980	1.00	22,278,000	1990	1.00
33,456,449	1980 D	1.00	20,096,242	1990 D	1.00
3,554,806	1980 S (proof only)		3,299,559	1990 S (proof only)	
29,544,000	1981	1.00	14,874,000	1991	1.00
27,839,533	1981 D	1.00	15,054,678	1991 D	1.00
4,063,083	1981 S (proof only)		2,867,787	1991 S (proof only)	
10,819,000	1982	1.00	17,628,000	1992	1.00
13,140,102	1982 D	1.00	17,000,106	1992 D	1.00
3,857,479	1982 S (proof only)		2,858,981	1992 S (proof only)	
34,139,000	1983	1.00	15,510,000	1993	1.00
32,472,244	1983 D	1.00	15,000,006	1993 D	1.00
3,228,648	1983 S (proof only)		2,633,439	1993 S (proof only)	
26,029,000	1984	1.00		1994	1.00
26,262,158	1984 D	1.00		1994 D	1.00
3,065,110	1984 S (proof only)			1994 S (proof only)	
18,706,962	1985	1.00		1995	1.00
19,814,034	1985 D	1.00		1995 D	1.00
3,362,662	1985 S (proof only)			1995 S (proof only)	
13,107,633	1986	1.00			
15,366,145	1986 D	1.00			
3,010,497	1986 S (proof only)				

Silver Dollars

DOLLARS—FLOWING HAIR TYPE

QUANTITY	YEAR	GOOD TO VERY GOOD	FINE	VERY FINE
1,758	1794 very rare	$6500.00	$15,000.00	$26,500.00
160,295	*1795	700.00	1100.00	2100.00

*This coin is included in quantity for 1795 draped bust type.

Silver Dollar—Flowing Hair Type

DOLLARS—DRAPED BUST TYPE

1795–1798   **1798–1804**

QUANTITY	YEAR	GOOD TO VERY GOOD	FINE	VERY FINE
184,013	1795	$600.00	$1200.00	$2000.00
72,920	1796	375.00	800.00	1300.00
7,776	1797 stars 10 and 6	500.00	1000.00	1400.00
	1797 stars 9 and 7	500.00	1000.00	1500.00
327,536	1798 small eagle, 15 stars	450.00	850.00	1250.00
	1798 small eagle, 13 stars	450.00	850.00	1250.00
327,536	1798 large eagle	400.00	750.00	1100.00
423,515	1799 over 98, 15 stars	400.00	750.00	1100.00
	1799 over 98, 13 stars	400.00	750.00	1000.00
	1799 stars 7 and 6	400.00	750.00	1000.00
	1799 stars 8 and 5	400.00	750.00	1000.00
220,920	1800	400.00	750.00	1000.00
54,454	1801	400.00	750.00	1000.00
41,650	1802 over 1	400.00	750.00	1000.00
	1802	400.00	700.00	950.00
66,064	1803	350.00	700.00	900.00
	1804 outstanding rarity			375,000.00

*A very rare 1804 Proof sold for $990,000.00 at a 7/7/89 auction

DOLLARS—LIBERTY SEATED TYPE

1840–1865   **1866–1873**

The mint marks are under the eagle on the reverse.

QUANTITY	YEAR	GOOD TO VERY GOOD	FINE	VERY FINE	EXT. FINE	UNC.
61,005	1840	$125.00	$175.00	$250.00	$375.00	$1400.00
173,000	1841	100.00	125.00	185.00	250.00	1000.00
184,618	1842	100.00	125.00	185.00	250.00	1000.00
165,100	1843	100.00	125.00	185.00	250.00	1000.00
20,000	1844	125.00	150.00	225.00	375.00	1750.00
24,500	1845	125.00	150.00	225.00	375.00	1750.00
110,600	1846	100.00	125.00	185.00	250.00	1000.00
59,000	1846 O	110.00	150.00	275.00	500.00	2500.00
140,750	1847	100.00	125.00	185.00	250.00	1000.00
15,000	1848	175.00	250.00	300.00	550.00	2250.00
62,600	1849	110.00	165.00	225.00	365.00	1500.00
7,500	1850	225.00	300.00	500.00	900.00	3750.00
40,000	1850 O	175.00	250.00	375.00	750.00	3500.00
1,300	1851	1300.00	2000.00	3250.00	6250.00	14,000.00
1,100	1852					12,500.00
46,110	1853	150.00	200.00	250.00	425.00	1500.00
33,140	1854	165.00	300.00	500.00	800.00	2750.00
26,000	1855	150.00	400.00	600.00	850.00	3000.00
63,500	1856	125.00	265.00	350.00	500.00	2250.00
94,000	1857	150.00	225.00	325.00	425.00	1800.00
80	1858	Struck in proof only, 7500.00				
256,500	1859	125.00	250.00	300.00	350.00	2000.00
360,000	1859 O	100.00	125.00	165.00	250.00	950.00
20,000	1859 S	175.00	300.00	425.00	750.00	3500.00
218,930	1860	100.00	125.00	200.00	325.00	1200.00
515,000	1860 O	90.00	115.00	150.00	250.00	900.00
78,500	1861	125.00	200.00	300.00	425.00	2000.00
12,090	1862	200.00	375.00	625.00	725.00	2000.00
27,660	1863	150.00	250.00	400.00	500.00	1750.00
31,170	1864	150.00	250.00	400.00	500.00	1750.00
47,000	1865	140.00	225.00	350.00	475.00	1700.00
49,625	1866 motto	140.00	225.00	350.00	475.00	1650.00
60,325	1867	140.00	225.00	350.00	475.00	1650.00
182,700	1868	125.00	200.00	275.00	375.00	1600.00
424,300	1869	120.00	175.00	225.00	300.00	1500.00
433,000	1870	120.00	175.00	225.00	300.00	1400.00
?	1870 S	Extremely rare	Stacks's Nov. 1989 Sale, VF, $77,000			
12,462	1870 CC	300.00	375.00	500.00	800.00	3000.00
1,115,760	1871	90.00	125.00	150.00	225.00	1100.00
1,376	1871 CC	700.00	1100.00	2000.00	3500.00	17,500.00
1,106,450	1872	100.00	125.00	175.00	300.00	1100.00
9,000	1872 S	200.00	350.00	500.00	850.00	3750.00
3,150	1872 CC	425.00	800.00	1500.00	1800.00	8500.00
293,600	1873	100.00	125.00	150.00	225.00	1250.00
2,300	1873 CC	1000.00	1750.00	2250.00	8500.00	22,500.00
700	1873 S	Extremely rare	Unknown in any collection			

DOLLARS—LIBERTY HEAD (MORGAN) TYPE

The mint mark is on the reverse under the eagle.

QUANTITY	YEAR	FINE	VERY FINE	EXT. FINE	UNC.	PROOF
10,509,550	1878 8 feathers	$14.00	$17.50	$22.50	$65.00	$1750.00
	1878 7 feathers		13.50	15.00	40.00	4500.00
	1878 7 over 8 feathers	20.00	25.00	28.00	65.00	
9,774,000	1878 S		16.50	18.50	50.00	
2,212,000	1878 CC	17.50	30.00	37.50	125.00	
14,807,100	1879		15.00	16.50	45.00	1750.00
2,887,000	1879 O	14.00	15.00	16.50	70.00	
9,110,000	1879 S		13.50	15.00	50.00	
756,000	1879 CC	35.00	75.00	225.00	1100.00	
12,601,355	1880		13.50	14.00	45.00	1750.00
5,305,000	1880 O	13.50	14.00	16.00	75.00	
8,900,000	1880 S		13.50	15.00	40.00	
591,000	1880 CC	50.00	65.00	85.00	150.00	
9,163,975	1881		13.50	15.00	40.00	1750.00
5,708,000	1881 O	13.50	15.00	16.00	40.00	
12,760,000	1881 S	13.50	15.00	16.00	40.00	
296,000	1881 CC	70.00	80.00	100.00	200.00	
11,101,100	1882		13.50	15.00	40.00	1750.00
6,090,000	1882 O	13.50	15.00	16.00	40.00	
9,250,000	1882 S		13.50	15.00	40.00	
1,133,000	1882 CC	25.00	35.00	40.00	100.00	
12,291,039	1883		13.50	15.00	40.00	1500.00
8,725,000	1883 O		13.50	14.00	30.00	
6,250,000	1883 S	15.00	17.50	27.50	400.00	
1,204,000	1883 CC	25.00	30.00	40.00	100.00	
14,070,875	1884		14.00	15.00	55.00	1500.00
9,730,000	1884 O		13.50	14.00	35.00	
3,200,000	1884 S	16.50	20.00	35.00	2000.00	
1,136,000	1884 CC	30.00	40.00	55.00	90.00	
17,787,767	1885		13.50	15.00	35.00	1500.00
9,185,000	1885 O		13.50	15.00	35.00	
1,497,000	1885 S	15.00	17.50	30.00	125.00	
228,000	1885 CC	125.00	150.00	175.00	265.00	
19,963,886	1886		13.50	15.00	37.50	1500.00
10,710,000	1886 O	14.00	15.00	20.00	350.00	
750,000	1886 S	20.00	24.00	28.00	200.00	
20,290,710	1887		13.50	14.00	30.00	1500.00
11,550,000	1887 O	14.00	15.00	16.00	55.00	
1,771,000	1887 S	15.00	17.50	25.00	90.00	
19,183,833	1888		13.50	15.00	35.00	1500.00
12,150,000	1888 O	14.00	15.00	17.50	35.00	
657,000	1888 S	25.00	27.50	35.00	175.00	
21,726,811	1889		14.00	17.50	35.00	1500.00
11,875,000	1889 O	$13.50	15.00	20.00	100.00	

DOLLARS—LIBERTY HEAD (MORGAN) TYPE (continued)

QUANTITY	YEAR	FINE	VERY FINE	EXT. FINE	UNC.	PROOF
700,000	1889 S	22.50	27.50	35.00	180.00	
350,000	1889 CC	150.00	250.00	550.00	7000.00	
16,802,590	1890		17.50	22.50	50.00	1650.00
10,701,000	1890 O	13.50	15.00	17.50	85.00	
8,230,373	1890 S	13.50	15.00	18.50	100.00	
2,309,041	1890 CC	25.00	35.00	50.00	250.00	
8,694,206	1891	14.00	16.00	17.50	100.00	1500.00
7,954,529	1891 O	14.00	16.00	25.00	150.00	
5,296,000	1891 S	14.00	16.50	17.50	100.00	
1,618,000	1891 CC	25.00	30.00	45.00	200.00	
1,037,245	1892	15.00	17.50	25.00	135.00	1500.00
2,744,000	1892 O	15.00	17.50	25.00	150.00	
1,200,000	1892 S	18.00	40.00	150.00	6250.00	
1,352,000	1892 CC	30.00	50.00	110.00	415.00	
378,792	1893	45.00	55.00	75.00	300.00	1750.00
300,000	1893 O	50.00	90.00	175.00	1000.00	
100,000	1893 S	650.00	1100.00	3500.00	26,500.00	
677,000	1893 CC	50.00	95.00	280.00	1100.00	
110,972	1894	225.00	350.00	475.00	1200.00	3250.00
1,723,000	1894 O	15.00	17.50	35.00	650.00	
1,260,000	1894 S	17.50	22.50	75.00	400.00	
12,880	1895 rare			8500.00	12,500.00	
450,000	1895 O	60.00	100.00	250.00	4500.00	
400,000	1895 S	80.00	150.00	375.00	1500.00	
9,976,762	1896	13.50	15.00	17.50	40.00	1500.00
4,900,000	1896 O	14.00	16.00	30.00	475.00	
5,000,000	1896 S	15.00	25.00	80.00	500.00	
2,822,731	1897	14.00	15.00	17.50	50.00	1500.00
4,004,000	1897 O	14.00	15.00	18.00	475.00	
5,825,000	1897 S	14.00	16.00	18.00	90.00	
5,884,735	1898	14.00	15.00	17.50	40.00	1500.00
4,440,000	1898 O	14.00	15.00	17.50	32.50	
4,102,000	1898 S	15.00	17.50	20.00	250.00	
330,846	1899	30.00	35.00	45.00	125.00	1500.00
12,290,000	1899 O		14.00	16.00	40.00	
2,562,000	1899 S	14.00	16.50	30.00	250.00	
8,830,912	1900		14.00	16.00	35.00	1250.00
12,590,000	1900 O		14.00	16.00	50.00	
3,540,000	1900 S	15.00	18.00	25.00	140.00	
6,962,813	1901	17.50	25.00	80.00	1000.00	2800.00
13,320,000	1901 O		14.00	16.00	35.00	
2,284,000	1901 S	15.00	18.00	25.00	320.00	
7,994,777	1902	14.00	16.00	17.50	70.00	1500.00
8,636,000	1902 O		14.00	16.00	30.00	
1,530,000	1902 S	32.50	50.00	75.00	250.00	
4,652,755	1903	15.00	17.50	22.50	70.00	1500.00
4,450,000	1903 O	90.00	125.00	140.00	300.00	
1,241,000	1903 S	18.00	25.00	200.00	1750.00	
2,788,650	1904	15.00	17.50	20.00	200.00	1500.00
3,720,000	1904 O	14.00	16.00	18.00	35.00	
2,304,000	1904 S	16.00	22.50	75.00	850.00	
44,690,000	1921			14.00	20.00	
21,695,000	1921 S			14.00	40.00	
20,345,000	1921 D			14.00	45.00	

DOLLARS—PEACE TYPE

QUANTITY	YEAR	VERY FINE	EXT. FINE	UNC.
1,006,473	1921	$30.00	$40.00	$200.00
51,737,000	1922	14.00	15.00	25.00
15,063,000	1922 D	14.00	15.00	30.00
17,475,000	1922 S	14.00	15.00	30.00
30,800,000	1923	14.00	15.00	17.50
6,811,000	1923 D	14.00	15.00	45.00
19,020,000	1923 S	14.00	15.00	50.00
11,811,000	1924	14.00	15.00	25.00

The mint marks are at the bottom to the left of the eagle's wing on the reverse.

QUANTITY	YEAR	VERY FINE	EXT. FINE	UNC.
1,728,000	1924 S	15.00	25.00	125.00
10,198,000	1925	14.00	15.00	25.00
1,610,000	1925 S	15.00	20.00	125.00
1,939,000	1926	14.00	16.50	30.00
2,348,700	1926 D	14.00	16.00	65.00
6,980,000	1926 S	14.00	16.00	40.00
848,000	1927	20.00	30.00	75.00
1,268,900	1927 D	15.00	25.00	200.00
866,000	1927 S	17.50	25.00	225.00
360,649	1928	125.00	150.00	250.00
1,632,000	1928 S	14.00	15.00	150.00
954,057	1934	17.50	25.00	75.00
1,569,000	1934 D	15.00	20.00	100.00
1,011,000	1934 S	40.00	150.00	1200.00
1,576,000	1935	15.00	20.00	55.00
1,964,000	1935 S	16.00	30.00	150.00

DOLLARS—EISENHOWER TYPE

QUANTITY	YEAR	MS-65	QUANTITY	YEAR	MS-65
47,799,000	1971	$2.75	2,000,056	1973	$12.50
68,587,424	1971 D	2.50	2,000,000	1973 D	12.50
6,668,526	1971 S	9.00	1,883,140	1973 S	10.00
75,890,000	1972	2.50	27,366,000	1974	2.35
95,548,511	1972 D	2.35	35,466,000	1974 D	2.35
2,193,056	1972 S	12.50	1,900,000	1974 S	12.50

DOLLARS—EISENHOWER TYPE (continued)

QUANTITY	YEAR	MS-65
4,019,000	1976 Copper-nickel clad, Variety I	$8.00
113,318,000	1976 Copper-nickel clad, Variety II	5.00
21,048,710	1976 D Copper-nickel clad, Variety I	6.00
82,179,564	1976 D Copper-nickel clad, Variety II	5.00
2,845,450	1976 S Copper-nickel clad, Variety I (proof)	
4,149,730	1976 S Copper-nickel clad, Variety II (proof)	
4,000,000	1976 S Silver clad, Variety I (proof)	
*4,149,730	1976 S Silver clad, Variety I	12.50
12,596,000	1977	2.35
32,983,006	1977 D	2.35
3,251,152	1977 S (proof only)	
25,702,000	1978	2.35
33,012,890	1978 D	2.35
3,127,781	1978 S (proof only)	

DOLLARS—SUSAN B. ANTHONY TYPE

QUANTITY	YEAR	MS-65
360,222,000	1979	1.75
288,015,744	1979 D	1.75
109,576,000	1979 S	1.75
3,677,175	1979 S (proof)	
27,610,000	1980	2.00
41,628,708	1980 D	2.00
20,422,000	1980 S	2.50
3,554,806	1980 S (proof)	
3,000,000	1981	5.00
3,250,000	1981 D	5.00
3,492,000	1981 S	5.00
4,063,083	1981 S (proof)	

Trade Dollars

These silver coins were issued from 1873 to 1885 for use in the Orient. From 1879 to 1885 Trade Dollars were issued only as proofs, apparently for collectors. It is said that Trade Dollars are still circulating in the Orient—some of them mutilated by "chopmarks" made to check their content.

TRADE DOLLARS

1873 —1885

The mint marks are under the eagle on the reverse.

QUANTITY	YEAR	GOOD TO VERY GOOD	FINE	VERY FINE	EXT. FINE	UNC.	PROOF
397,500	1873	$55.00	$70.00	$85.00	$125.00	$700.00	$2750.00
703,000	1873 S	55.00	70.00	100.00	150.00	750.00	
124,500	1873 CC	60.00	80.00	120.00	350.00	1250.00	
987,800	1874	55.00	70.00	80.00	130.00	700.00	2750.00
2,549,000	1874 S	55.00	60.00	70.00	100.00	550.00	
1,373,200	1874 CC	60.00	70.00	80.00	120.00	800.00	
218,900	1875	75.00	100.00	200.00	300.00	1200.00	2750.00
4,487,000	1875 S	55.00	60.00	70.00	120.00	600.00	
1,573,700	1875 CC	60.00	70.00	85.00	130.00	700.00	
456,150	1876	55.00	70.00	80.00	120.00	650.00	2750.00
5,227,000	1876 S	55.00	60.00	70.00	100.00	550.00	
509,000	1876 CC	60.00	70.00	100.00	200.00	1000.00	
3,039,710	1877	55.00	60.00	70.00	100.00	600.00	2750.00
9,519,000	1877 S	55.00	60.00	70.00	100.00	575.00	
534,000	1877 CC	65.00	100.00	130.00	250.00	1100.00	
900	1878 Proofs only						3000.00
4,162,000	1878 S	55.00	60.00	75.00	100.00	550.00	
97,000	1878 CC	200.00	325.00	500.00	850.00	5500.00	
1,541	1879 Proofs only						3000.00
1,987	1880 Proofs only						3000.00
960	1881 Proofs only						3000.00
1,097	1882 Proofs only						3000.00
979	1883 Proofs only						3000.00
10	1884 Proofs only						75,000.00
5	1885 Proofs only						165,000.00

GOLD COINS

There are a number of reasons why gold coins are scarce and have substantial values. Gold is intrinsically much more valuable than silver, and there have been times when it was desirable to melt down gold coins for what the metal would bring.

Remember, also, that up to the time gold was discovered in California in 1848, the metal was scarce in the United States. Consequently the early issues of gold coins were small and the coins correspondingly scarce. Then, too, gold coins never circulated to more than a very limited extent; collectors did not come across these coins in ordinary usage.

Still another reason for the present-day scarcity of gold coins is the Presidential Order of 1933 which removed gold coins from circulation. (The order, by the way, made a careful distinction in favor of coin collectors by allowing them to continue acquiring gold coins as part of their hobby.)

Gold coins were struck in the following denominations:

Gold Dollars	1849–1889
Quarter Eagles ($2.50)	1796–1929
Three-Dollar Gold Pieces	1854–1889
Half Eagles ($5)	1795–1929
Eagles ($10)	1795–1933
Double Eagles ($20)	1849–1933

New interpretations and amendments concerning the 1933 order were issued beginning in 1954 until finally all restrictions on ownership of gold were removed as of January 1975. U.S. citizens may now buy, sell, or hold gold in any form.

After a lapse of more than 50 years, the United States resumed gold coinage in 1984 with a $10 denomination commemorating the 1984 Los Angeles Summer Olympics. A $5 gold coin was released in 1986 to commemorate the centennial of the Statue of Liberty.

Additional $5 cold coin commemoratives were issued to mark the 1987 Constitutional Bicentennial, the 1988 Seoul Olympics, the 1989 Congress Bicentennial, the 1991 Mount Rushmore Golden Anniversary, the 1992 Barcelona Summer Olympics, the 1992 Columbus 500th Anniversary, the 1993 Bill of Rights Bicentennial, the 1994 World Cup Soccer Tournament and for the 1996 Atlanta Summer Olympics, among others.

Gold Dollars

These coins were first issued when gold became plentiful after the California Gold Rush. They are very small, weighing only 25.8 grains. (A silver dollar weighs over 400 grains.) Due to the highly unpredictable and volatile nature of the current precious metals markets, prices for gold and silver coins may fluctuate significantly.

LIBERTY HEAD TYPE

QUANTITY	YEAR	FINE	VERY FINE	UNC.
658,567	1849 open wreath—			
	small head and stars	$125.00	$200.00	$600.00
	1849 open wreath—			
	large head and stars	125.00	200.00	600.00
	1849 closed wreath	200.00	300.00	650.00
?	1849 C open wreath (extremely rare)		100,000.00	
11,634	1849 C closed wreath	275.00	550.00	3750.00
21,588	1849 D open wreath	285.00	575.00	4250.00
215,000	1849 O open wreath	225.00	350.00	900.00
481,953	1850	150.00	225.00	600.00
6,966	1850 C	375.00	675.00	5500.00
8,382	1850 D	365.00	650.00	5000.00
14,000	1850 O	250.00	325.00	2250.00
3,317,671	1851	150.00	200.00	600.00
41,267	1851 C	275.00	450.00	2250.00
9,882	1851 D	300.00	475.00	3500.00
290,000	1851 O	175.00	225.00	725.00
2,045,351	1852	125.00	200.00	550.00
9,434	1852 C	285.00	475.00	3250.00
6,360	1852 D	325.00	625.00	5000.00
140,000	1852 O	150.00	250.00	850.00
4,076,051	1853	150.00	250.00	550.00
11,515	1853 C	265.00	500.00	5250.00
6,583	1853 D	350.00	625.00	6500.00
290,000	1853 O	150.00	275.00	750.00
1,639,445*	1854	140.00	225.00	500.00
2,935	1854 D	550.00	825.00	12,500.00
14,632	1854 S	300.00	425.00	2100.00

*includes Indian-Headdress Dollars of 1854

INDIAN-HEADDRESS TYPE

QUANTITY	YEAR	FINE	VERY FINE	UNC.
783,943	1854	200.00	375.00	3250.00
758,269	1855	200.00	350.00	3250.00
9,803	1855 C	650.00	1100.00	12,000.00
1,811	1855 D	1900.00	3250.00	22,500.00
55,000	1855 O	400.00	600.00	6000.00
24,600	1856 S	450.00	700.00	7250.00

LARGER INDIAN-HEADDRESS TYPE

1,762,936	1856	150.00	225.00	600.00
1,460	1856 D	2500.00	4000.00	22,500.00

LARGER INDIAN-HEADDRESS TYPE (continued)

QUANTITY	YEAR	FINE	VERY FINE	UNC.
774,789	1857	$150.00	$200.00	$425.00
13,280	1857 C	300.00	525.00	5500.00
3,533	1857 D	500.00	850.00	8500.00
10,000	1857 S	350.00	550.00	6250.00
117,995	1858	175.00	225.00	625.00
3,477	1858 D	600.00	875.00	7250.00
10,000	1858 S	325.00	450.00	3750.00
168,244	1859	175.00	200.00	500.00
5,235	1859 C	375.00	600.00	7500.00
4,952	1859 D	500.00	800.00	7500.00
15,000	1859 S	300.00	425.00	5500.00
36,668	1860	175.00	250.00	550.00
1,556	1860 D	2300.00	2750.00	25,000.00
13,000	1860 S	300.00	375.00	3250.00
527,499	1861	150.00	225.00	600.00
?	1861 D	5000.00	7250.00	32,500.00
1,326,865	1862	185.00	200.00	500.00
6,250	1863	325.00	475.00	3750.00
5,950	1864	325.00	425.00	1750.00
3,725	1865	325.00	425.00	2000.00
7,180	1866	300.00	425.00	1300.00
5,250	1867	300.00	450.00	1500.00
10,525	1868	250.00	325.00	1200.00
5,925	1869	285.00	425.00	1300.00
6,335	1870	275.00	350.00	1200.00
3,000	1870 S	300.00	600.00	3250.00
3,930	1871	285.00	425.00	1100.00
3,530	1872	285.00	425.00	1100.00
125,125	1873	225.00	350.00	750.00
198,820	1874	150.00	225.00	450.00
420	1875	2000.00	3000.00	8500.00
3,425	1876	200.00	325.00	1100.00
3,920	1877	250.00	400.00	1000.00
3,020	1878	225.00	350.00	1100.00
3,030	1879	225.00	350.00	1000.00
1,636	1880	200.00	300.00	1000.00
7,660	1881	200.00	300.00	800.00
5,040	1882	200.00	300.00	800.00
10,840	1883	150.00	250.00	625.00
6,206	1884	175.00	275.00	650.00
12,205	1885	150.00	250.00	650.00
6,016	1886	175.00	275.00	650.00
8,543	1887	175.00	275.00	650.00
16,080	1888	175.00	275.00	650.00
30,729	1889	175.00	275.00	650.00

Quarter Eagles ($2.50)

The handsome Indian Head Type in the quarter eagle and half eagle series is unique in United States coinage in that the design and legends are incused. This means they are sunk below the surface of the coin instead of being in relief (raised above the surface of the coin).

LIBERTY CAP TYPE

LIBERTY CAP TYPE

QUANTITY	YEAR	FINE	VERY FINE	UNC.
963	1796 no stars	$9000.00	$15,000.00	$85,000.00
432	1796 with stars	7500.00	13,500.00	60,000.00
1,756	1797	5000.00	9000.00	37,500.00
614	1798	3500.00	5000.00	20,000.00
2,612	1802 over 1	2500.00	3750.00	16,500.00
3,327	1804	2750.00	4000.00	18,500.00
1,781	1805	2500.00	3500.00	16,000.00
1,616	1806 over 4	2500.00	3250.00	17,000.00
	1806 over 5	4000.00	7500.00	25,000.00
6,812	1807	2500.00	3250.00	16,000.00

LIBERTY HEAD WITH MOTTO OVER EAGLE

2,710	1808	6500.00	13,000.00	40,000.00
6,448	1821 reduced size	2000.00	3500.00	14,000.00
2,600	1824 over 21	2000.00	3750.00	15,000.00
4,434	1825	2000.00	3750.00	14,000.00
760	1826 over 25	3000.00	5500.00	22,500.00
2,800	1827	2000.00	3000.00	15,500.00
3,403	1829	2000.00	3000.00	12,000.00
4,540	1830	2000.00	3000.00	12,000.00
4,520	1831	2000.00	3000.00	12,000.00
4,400	1832	2000.00	3000.00	12,000.00
4,160	1833	2000.00	3000.00	12,000.00
4,000	1834	3750.00	5500.00	28,500.00

RIBBON TYPE WITHOUT MOTTO

The mint mark—only on 1838 and 1839—is above the date on the obverse.

112,324	1834	200.00	285.00	2400.00
131,402	1835	200.00	285.00	2250.00
547,986	1836	200.00	285.00	2250.00
45,080	1837	225.00	300.00	2300.00
47,030	1838	225.00	300.00	2300.00
7,908	1838 C	550.00	850.00	15,000.00
27,021	1839	225.00	300.00	3750.00
18,173	1839 C	500.00	750.00	10,000.00
13,674	1839 D	500.00	800.00	10,500.00
17,781	1839 O	400.00	600.00	5750.00

QUARTER EAGLES–CORONET TYPE WITHOUT MOTTO

The mint mark is below the eagle on the reverse.

QUANTITY	YEAR	FINE	VERY FINE	UNC.
18,859	1840	$175.00	$250.00	$2750.00
12,838	1840 C	285.00	525.00	8500.00
3,532	1840 D	400.00	800.00	12,500.00
26,200	1840 O	250.00	500.00	4500.00
?	1841	(an outstanding rarity; Proof $100,000.00)		
10,297	1841 C	325.00	525.00	7500.00
4,164	1841 D	400.00	1000.00	12,000.00
2,823	1842	375.00	875.00	12,500.00
6,737	1842 C	375.00	800.00	10,000.00
4,643	1842 D	375.00	1000.00	12,500.00
19,800	1842 O	300.00	525.00	7500.00
100,546	1843	200.00	375.00	1400.00
26,096	1843 C	375.00	625.00	6500.00
36,209	1843 D	325.00	600.00	5000.00
368,002	1843 O	175.00	275.00	1250.00
6,784	1844	275.00	500.00	5250.00
11,622	1844 C	275.00	575.00	7500.00
17,732	1844 D	275.00	500.00	6250.00
91,051	1845	200.00	285.00	1000.00
19,460	1845 D	350.00	600.00	7500.00
4,000	1845 O	625.00	1100.00	13,500.00
21,598	1846	200.00	400.00	2750.00
4,808	1846 C	550.00	850.00	10,000.00
19,303	1846 D	325.00	725.00	7000.00
66,000	1846 O	250.00	325.00	2500.00
29,814	1847	200.00	300.00	2250.00
23,226	1847 C	300.00	525.00	5000.00
15,784	1847 D	375.00	575.00	6250.00
124,000	1847 O	185.00	325.00	2250.00
8,886	1848	400.00	750.00	5250.00
	1848 CAL over eagle (rare)	4500.00	6500.00	32,000.00
16,788	1848 C	450.00	625.00	6750.00
13,771	1848 D	500.00	650.00	7250.00
23,294	1849	225.00	350.00	1750.00
10,220	1849 C	425.00	625.00	8250.00
10,945	1849 D	425.00	700.00	8500.00
252,923	1850	175.00	250.00	850.00
9,148	1850 C	400.00	600.00	8250.00
12,148	1850 D	325.00	500.00	5000.00
84,000	1850 O	275.00	325.00	2500.00
1,372,648	1851	175.00	235.00	700.00
14,923	1851 C	325.00	550.00	7500.00
11,264	1851 D	325.00	550.00	7500.00
148,000	1851 O	250.00	275.00	2250.00
1,159,681	1852	175.00	235.00	1750.00
9,772	1852 C	425.00	575.00	7000.00
4,078	1852 D	525.00	775.00	9000.00
140,000	1852 O	175.00	250.00	2750.00
1,404,668	1853	150.00	200.00	750.00
3,178	1853 D	625.00	1000.00	10,000.00
596,258	1854	175.00	235.00	625.00
7,295	1854 C	375.00	625.00	8000.00
1,760	1854 D	1400.00	3000.00	14,000.00
153,000	1854 O	175.00	285.00	1250.00

QUANTITY	YEAR	FINE	VERY FINE	UNC.
246	1854 S	13,000.00	27,500.00	75,000.00
235,480	1855	175.00	250.00	625.00
3,677	1855 C	750.00	1100.00	12,500.00
1,123	1855 D	1500.00	3500.00	20,000.00
384,240	1856	150.00	200.00	600.00
7,913	1856 C	475.00	750.00	10,000.00
874	1856 D	4000.00	7250.00	35,000.00
21,100	1856 O	175.00	250.00	2750.00
71,120	1856 S	175.00	265.00	2250.00
214,130	1857	165.00	235.00	600.00
2,364	1857 D	475.00	900.00	8500.00
34,000	1857 O	200.00	325.00	2850.00
68,000	1857 S	175.00	250.00	3000.00
47,377	1858	175.00	250.00	1250.00
9,056	1858 C	315.00	625.00	7500.00
39,444	1859	175.00	250.00	1250.00
2,244	1859 D	550.00	1250.00	10,000.00
15,200	1859 S	250.00	425.00	5000.00
22,675	1860	200.00	300.00	1100.00
7,469	1860 C	350.00	650.00	7500.00
35,600	1860 S	180.00	300.00	2750.00
1,272,518	1861	180.00	250.00	625.00
24,000	1861 S	250.00	375.00	2500.00
112,353	1862	175.00	250.00	1000.00
8,000	1862 S	400.00	750.00	9250.00
30	* 1863 very rare			
10,800	1863 S	225.00	425.00	5000.00
2,874	1864	1000.00	2500.00	17,500.00
1,545	1865	525.00	2500.00	16,500.00
23,376	1865 S	200.00	275.00	2850.00
3,110	1866	425.00	900.00	8000.00
38,960	1866 S	200.00	350.00	2750.00
3,250	1867	350.00	625.00	7250.00
28,000	1867 S	225.00	325.00	2750.00
3,625	1868	300.00	425.00	2500.00
34,000	1868 S	175.00	250.00	2750.00
4,345	1869	300.00	325.00	3000.00
29,500	1869 S	175.00	250.00	2750.00
4,555	1870	250.00	350.00	3000.00
16,000	1870 S	185.00	275.00	2500.00
5,350	1871	225.00	375.00	2800.00
22,000	1871 S	175.00	250.00	1750.00
3,030	1872	275.00	400.00	4500.00
178,025	1873	175.00	225.00	800.00
27,000	1873 S	185.00	250.00	1750.00
3,940	1874	235.00	325.00	3200.00
420	1875	1750.00	4500.00	18,500.00
11,600	1875 S	175.00	250.00	2000.00
4,221	1876	250.00	325.00	2800.00
5,000	1876 S	225.00	300.00	2000.00
1,652	1877	340.00	550.00	3750.00
35,400	1877 S	180.00	225.00	750.00
286,260	1878	165.00	215.00	500.00
178,000	1878 S	165.00	215.00	500.00
88,900	1879	165.00	215.00	500.00
43,500	1879 S	175.00	225.00	800.00
2,996	1880	250.00	325.00	1200.00
680	1881	600.00	1200.00	11,000.00
4,040	1882	250.00	300.00	1200.00
1,960	1883	225.00	275.00	1300.00
1,993	1884	225.00	300.00	1500.00
887	1885	500.00	750.00	5250.00
4,088	1886	200.00	275.00	1250.00
6,282	1887	175.00	250.00	1000.00
16,098	1888	150.00	225.00	700.00
17,648	1889	150.00	225.00	625.00
8,813	1890	165.00	250.00	700.00

* Proof-63 specimen sold for $80,000 at Aug. 1990 RARCOA auction.

QUARTER EAGLES ; CORONET TYPE WITHOUT MOTTO (continued)

QUANTITY	YEAR	FINE	VERY FINE	UNC.
11,040	1891	150.00	225.00	600.00
2,545	1892	200.00	275.00	1000.00
30,106	1893	150.00	225.00	500.00
4,122	1894	165.00	275.00	850.00
6,119	1895	165.00	275.00	625.00
19,202	1896	150.00	200.00	500.00
29,904	1897	150.00	200.00	500.00
24,165	1898	150.00	200.00	500.00
27,350	1899	150.00	200.00	500.00
67,205	1900	150.00	200.00	500.00
91,323	1901	150.00	200.00	500.00
133,733	1902	150.00	200.00	500.00
201,257	1903	150.00	200.00	500.00
160,960	1904	150.00	200.00	500.00
217,944	1905	150.00	200.00	500.00
176,490	1906	150.00	200.00	500.00
336,448	1907	150.00	200.00	500.00

INDIAN HEAD INCUSE TYPE

The mint mark is to the left of the eagle's claw on the reverse.

QUANTITY	YEAR	VERY FINE	EXT. FINE	UNC.
565,057	1908	$150.00	$200.00	$325.00
441,899	1909	150.00	200.00	340.00
492,682	1910	150.00	200.00	340.00
704,191	1911	150.00	200.00	340.00
55,680	1911 D	625.00	1000.00	3000.00
616,197	1912	150.00	200.00	340.00
722,165	1913	150.00	200.00	340.00
240,117	1914	150.00	200.00	375.00
448,000	1914 D	150.00	200.00	340.00
606,100	1915	150.00	200.00	340.00
578,000	1925 D	150.00	200.00	340.00
446,000	1926	150.00	200.00	340.00
388,000	1927	150.00	200.00	340.00
416,000	1928	150.00	200.00	340.00
532,000	1929	150.00	200.00	340.00

Three-Dollar Gold Pieces

Like the three-cent pieces, these coins were intended for buying three-cent stamps. However, the public remained indifferent to both types of coins. When the postal rate was changed, the coinage of these gold pieces came to an end.

THREE-DOLLAR GOLD PIECES

The mint mark is below the wreath on the reverse.

QUANTITY	YEAR	FINE	VERY FINE	UNC.
138,618	1854	$400.00	$625.00	$2500.00
1,120	1854 D	4000.00	6500.00	25,000.00
24,000	1854 O	475.00	675.00	3250.00
50,555	1855	450.00	625.00	3000.00
6,600	1855 S	600.00	1000.00	10,000.00
26,010	1856	450.00	600.00	2750.00
34,500	1856 S small S	450.00	650.00	3750.00
20,891	1857	450.00	800.00	3000.00
14,000	1857 S	550.00	825.00	6500.00
2,133	1858	550.00	800.00	5000.00
15,638	1859	450.00	750.00	3000.00
7,155	1860	465.00	800.00	3250.00
7,000	1860 S	550.00	800.00	6500.00
6,072	1861	550.00	750.00	3750.00
5,785	1862	550.00	700.00	3750.00
5,039	1863	550.00	800.00	4000.00
2,680	1864	550.00	800.00	4000.00
1,165	1865	625.00	825.00	7250.00
4,030	1866	500.00	700.00	4500.00
2,650	1867	600.00	850.00	4750.00
4,875	1868	550.00	700.00	4250.00
2,525	1869	575.00	850.00	4750.00
3,535	1870	550.00	750.00	4000.00
2	1870 S unique $687,500, Bowers & Ruddy Oct. 1982 "U.S. Gold Sale"			
1,330	1871	650.00	850.00	4500.00
2,030	1872	575.00	750.00	4250.00
25	1873 (only proofs were struck)			32,500.00
41,820	1874	425.00	550.00	3250.00
20	1875 (only proofs were struck) $159,000, RARCOA Aug. 1990 Sale			
45	1876 (only proofs were struck) $35,200 1984 Carter Sale			
1,488	1877	750.00	1100.00	7500.00
82,234	1878	375.00	550.00	2750.00
3,030	1879	450.00	750.00	3750.00
1,036	1880	500.00	800.00	4250.00
550	1881	800.00	1000.00	5000.00
1,540	1882	500.00	575.00	4250.00
940	1883	575.00	825.00	4500.00
1,106	1884	575.00	800.00	4750.00
910	1885	575.00	800.00	4750.00
1,142	1886	550.00	750.00	4000.00
6,160	1887	500.00	750.00	3000.00
5,291	1888	500.00	750.00	3000.00
2,429	1889	500.00	750.00	3000.00

Four-Dollar Gold Pieces

These coins are sometimes called "Stellas" because of the star on the obverse. Though struck as patterns in 1879 and 1880, they were never issued as regular coins. The decision not to use them was a sensible one, as three-dollar and five-dollar gold pieces were already in existence.

The "Stellas" were struck in very small quantities and are therefore among the highly prized rarities of American coinage.

FOUR-DOLLAR ("STELLA") GOLD PIECE PATTERNS

(only proofs were struck)

QUANTITY	YEAR	PROOF-63
415	1879 flowing hair	$55,000.00
10	1879 coiled hair	130,000.00
15	1880 flowing hair	75,000.00
10	1880 coiled hair	150,000.00

Half Eagles ($5)

It is curious that up to 1807 these coins carried no indication of their value.

BUST TYPE FACING RIGHT

1795–1798   1795–1807

Half Eagles ($5 Gold Pieces)

QUANTITY	YEAR	FINE	VERY FINE	UNC.
8,707	1795 small eagle	$5000.00	$8500.00	$27,500.00
	1795 large eagle	5500.00	9000.00	37,500.00
3,399	1796 over 95 small eagle	6000.00	10,000.00	37,500.00
6,406	1797 over 95 large eagle	5000.00	8000.00	27,500.00
	1797 15 stars small eagle	6000.00	10,000.00	37,500.00
	1797 16 stars small eagle	5500.00	9000.00	32,500.00
24,867	1798 small eagle	6500.00	20,000.00	50,000.00
	1798 large eagle	2500.00	3000.00	15,000.00
7,451	1799	1000.00	2000.00	10,000.00
11,622	1800	1000.00	1750.00	8500.00
53,176	1802 over 1	1000.00	1750.00	8000.00
33,506	1803 over 2	1000.00	1750.00	8000.00
30,475	1804	1100.00	1750.00	8000.00
33,183	1805	1100.00	1850.00	9000.00
64,093	1806	1100.00	1800.00	8500.00
33,496	1807	1000.00	1800.00	8500.00

BUST TYPE FACING LEFT

1807–1812   **1813–1834**

QUANTITY	YEAR	FINE	VERY FINE	UNC.
50,597	1807	1100.00	1500.00	8000.00
55,578	1808 over 7	1200.00	1650.00	8500.00
	1808	1100.00	1400.00	8000.00
33,875	1809 over 8	1100.00	1400.00	8000.00
	1809	1100.00	1400.00	8000.00
100,287	1810	1100.00	1500.00	8500.00
99,581	1811	1100.00	1500.00	8500.00
58,087	1812	1000.00	1400.00	8000.00
95,428	1813 larger head	1100.00	1400.00	8750.00
15,454	1814	1750.00	2800.00	12,500.00
635	1815		65,000.00	125,000.00
45,588	1818	1500.00	2500.00	10,000.00
51,723	1819	7500.00	10,000.00	45,000.00
263,806	1820	1250.00	2000.00	10,000.00
34,641	1821	3000.00	6250.00	20,000.00
17,796	1822 an outstanding rarity; proof			687,500.00
14,485	1823	2750.00	4250.00	15,000.00
17,340	1824	4500.00	8000.00	32,500.00
29,060	1825 over 21	4000.00	6500.00	24,000.00
	1825 over 24 $148,500 Bowers & Merena, March 1989 Sale			
18,069	1826	5000.00	5500.00	20,000.00
24,913	1827	10,000.00	20,000.00	50,000.00
28,029	1828 over 27	5000.00	7000.00	20,000.00
	1828	7500.00	10,000.00	28,500.00
57,442	1829 $104,500, Superior July 1985 Sale			
126,351	1830	2250.00	3650.00	16,500.00
140,594	1831	2250.00	3650.00	16,500.00
157,487	1832 curled 2, 12 stars	5500.00	7500.00	25,000.00
	1832 square-based 2, 13 stars	3500.00	6750.00	20,000.00
193,630	1833	2200.00	3750.00	16,000.00
50,141	1834	2250.00	3800.00	15,000.00

RIBBON TYPE WITHOUT MOTTO

The mint mark—only on 1838—is above the date on the obverse.

QUANTITY	YEAR	FINE	VERY FINE	UNC.
682,028	1834	250.00	300.00	3000.00
371,534	1835	235.00	285.00	3000.00
553,147	1836	235.00	285.00	3000.00
207,121	1837	265.00	325.00	3250.00

HALF EAGLES: RIBBON TYPE WITHOUT MOTTO (continued)

QUANTITY	YEAR	FINE	VERY FINE	UNC.
286,588	1838	265.00	325.00	3250.00
12,913	1838 C	800.00	1250.00	6500.00
20,583	1838 D	800.00	1250.00	7000.00

CORONET TYPE

1839–1865   **1866–1908**

The mint mark is below the eagle on the reverse.

118,143	1839	235.00	300.00	3250.00
17,205	1839 C	475.00	800.00	8500.00
18,939	1839 D	475.00	800.00	7500.00
137,382	1840	225.00	265.00	3500.00
19,028	1840 C	500.00	750.00	8250.00
22,896	1840 D	500.00	750.00	8250.00
30,400	1840 O	300.00	475.00	6250.00
15,833	1841	275.00	450.00	4750.00
21,511	1841 C	425.00	650.00	8750.00
30,495	1841 D	425.00	650.00	8500.00
8,350	1841 O (2 known)			
27,578	1842	225.00	325.00	4500.00
27,480	1842 C	375.00	700.00	7500.00
59,608	1842 D	375.00	700.00	6500.00
16,400	1842 O	325.00	500.00	5000.00
611,205	1843	185.00	200.00	1750.00
44,353	1843 C	400.00	650.00	5000.00
98,452	1843 D	350.00	550.00	6250.00
101,075	1843 O	250.00	375.00	3750.00
340,330	1844	185.00	200.00	1850.00
23,631	1844 C	375.00	625.00	6750.00
88,982	1844 D	375.00	575.00	7000.00
364,600	1844 O	250.00	400.00	3750.00
417,099	1845	200.00	250.00	2000.00
90,629	1845 D	325.00	500.00	5000.00
41,000	1845 O	275.00	475.00	4500.00
395,942	1846	200.00	225.00	2000.00
12,995	1846 C	400.00	750.00	7500.00
80,294	1846 D	350.00	600.00	6750.00
58,000	1846 O	275.00	425.00	5000.00
915,981	1847	200.00	225.00	1750.00
84,151	1847 C	375.00	600.00	5250.00
64,405	1847 D	375.00	600.00	5500.00
12,000	1847 O	450.00	700.00	6750.00
260,775	1848	200.00	250.00	1800.00
64,472	1848 C	400.00	625.00	6000.00
47,465	1848 D	400.00	625.00	6250.00
133,070	1849	200.00	250.00	2250.00
64,823	1849 C	400.00	600.00	6500.00
39,036	1849 D	400.00	600.00	6500.00
64,491	1850	250.00	325.00	3750.00
63,591	1850 C	400.00	525.00	5500.00
43,950	1850 D	400.00	525.00	6250.00
377,505	1851	200.00	250.00	1800.00
49,176	1851 C	400.00	500.00	5750.00
62,710	1851 D	400.00	500.00	5750.00

QUANTITY	YEAR	FINE	VERY FINE	UNC.
41,000	1851 O	350.00	550.00	4250.00
573,901	1852	180.00	200.00	1500.00
72,574	1852 C	375.00	550.00	5500.00
91,452	1852 D	375.00	550.00	5000.00
305,770	1853	180.00	235.00	1850.00
65,571	1853 C	375.00	550.00	5000.00
89,678	1853 D	375.00	500.00	5000.00
160,675	1854	180.00	250.00	1800.00
39,291	1854 C	400.00	550.00	5750.00
56,413	1854 D	375.00	525.00	5000.00
46,000	1854 O	265.00	450.00	3850.00
268	1854 S	ext. rare Sold for $210,000.00 at 1983 auction		
117,098	1855	180.00	235.00	1650.00
39,788	1855 C	400.00	550.00	4500.00
22,432	1855 D	400.00	550.00	5000.00
11,100	1855 O	425.00	575.00	6250.00
61,000	1855 S	215.00	375.00	3750.00
197,990	1856	180.00	200.00	1650.00
28,457	1856 C	425.00	550.00	4750.00
19,786	1856 D	425.00	550.00	5000.00
10,000	1856 O	425.00	625.00	7250.00
105,100	1856 S	250.00	300.00	3850.00
98,188	1857	180.00	225.00	1850.00
31,360	1857 C	375.00	600.00	6000.00
17,046	1857 D	425.00	625.00	6750.00
13,000	1857 O	350.00	575.00	5750.00
87,000	1857 S	215.00	300.00	3250.00
15,136	1858	250.00	350.00	3000.00
38,856	1858 C	375.00	550.00	5000.00
15,362	1858 D	375.00	550.00	5500.00
18,600	1858 S	325.00	525.00	4250.00
16,814	1859	250.00	375.00	3500.00
31,847	1859 C	375.00	525.00	5000.00
10,366	1859 D	425.00	575.00	6250.00
13,220	1859 S	450.00	550.00	6000.00
19,825	1860	250.00	375.00	3750.00
14,813	1860 C	375.00	625.00	7500.00
14,635	1860 D	375.00	625.00	9000.00
21,200	1860 S	350.00	600.00	8500.00
639,950	1861	185.00	250.00	1650.00
6,879	1861 C	1000.00	1500.00	12,500.00
1,597	1861 D	3250.00	5000.00	27,500.00
18,000	1861 S	325.00	625.00	7500.00
4,465	1862	475.00	750.00	7500.00
9,500	1862 S	550.00	850.00	8500.00
2,472	1863	650.00	1000.00	10,000.00
17,000	1863 S	375.00	800.00	6850.00
4,220	1864	450.00	625.00	8250.00
3,888	1864 S	1300.00	2850.00	16,500.00
1,295	1865	575.00	1000.00	10,000.00
27,612	1865 S	375.00	800.00	8500.00
43,920*	1866 S no motto	400.00	1000.00	9500.00

CORONET TYPE WITH MOTTO

The mint mark is below the eagle on the reverse.

6,730	1866	375.00	525.00	3750.00
34,920	*1866 S	350.00	500.00	3500.00
6,920	1867	350.00	500.00	3000.00
29,000	1867 S	275.00	450.00	3000.00
5,725	1868	325.00	500.00	6250.00
52,000	1868 S	275.00	425.00	3750.00
1,785	1869	600.00	850.00	7250.00
31,000	1869 S	325.00	625.00	3750.00
4,035	1870	350.00	650.00	5750.00
7,675	1870 CC	1400.00	2500.00	17,500.00

*Includes 1866 S coins with motto.

HALF EAGLES: CORONET TYPE WITH MOTTO (continued)

QUANTITY	YEAR	FINE	VERY FINE	UNC.
17,000	1870 S	325.00	500.00	4250.00
3,230	1871	375.00	625.00	4250.00
20,770	1871 CC	525.00	825.00	7250.00
25,000	1871 S	300.00	500.00	4000.00
1,690	1872	500.00	725.00	4500.00
16,980	1872 CC	500.00	800.00	4750.00
36,400	1872 S	275.00	450.00	3850.00
112,505	1873	200.00	300.00	1100.00
7,416	1873 CC	625.00	1100.00	7500.00
31,000	1873 S	350.00	525.00	3750.00
3,508	1874	375.00	600.00	4750.00
21,198	1874 CC	375.00	600.00	5500.00
16,000	1874 S	325.00	525.00	5000.00
220	1875	rare $115,000, Akers 1990 Sale, Proof		
11,828	1875 CC	525.00	900.00	8250.00
9,000	1875 S	325.00	625.00	4750.00
1,477	1876	525.00	1000.00	8500.00
6,887	1876 CC	500.00	800.00	5750.00
4,000	1876 S	500.00	800.00	6500.00
1,152	1877	625.00	1000.00	9000.00
8,680	1877 CC	500.00	900.00	5750.00
26,700	1877 S	250.00	325.00	2000.00
131,740	1878	180.00	200.00	650.00
9,054	1878 CC	875.00	1600.00	13,500.00
144,700	1878 S	185.00	225.00	875.00
301,950	1879	175.00	200.00	500.00
17,281	1879 CC	300.00	400.00	3750.00
426,200	1879 S	200.00	250.00	625.00
3,166,436	1880	175.00	200.00	365.00
51,017	1880 CC	275.00	525.00	2850.00
1,348,900	1880 S	200.00	275.00	385.00
5,708,800	1881	175.00	200.00	300.00
13,886	1881 CC	325.00	500.00	4250.00
969,000	1881 S	175.00	200.00	365.00
2,514,560	1882	175.00	200.00	365.00
82,817	1882 CC	225.00	325.00	2250.00
969,000	1882 S	175.00	200.00	365.00
233,440	1883	175.00	200.00	365.00
12,598	1883 CC	250.00	425.00	2850.00
83,200	1883 S	200.00	275.00	825.00
191,048	1884	185.00	215.00	750.00
16,402	1884 CC	250.00	525.00	2750.00
177,000	1884 S	175.00	225.00	525.00
601,506	1885	175.00	200.00	375.00
1,211,500	1885 S	175.00	200.00	375.00
388,432	1886	175.00	200.00	375.00
3,268,000	1886 S	175.00	200.00	375.00
87	1887	rare (only proofs were struck) 28,500.00		
1,912,000	1887 S	175.00	225.00	365.00
18,296	1888	200.00	275.00	750.00
293,900	1888 S	200.00	275.00	1000.00
7,565	1889	300.00	400.00	1100.00
4,328	1890	325.00	550.00	1850.00
53,800	1890 CC	200.00	285.00	1100.00
61,413	1891	175.00	225.00	650.00
208,000	1891 CC	200.00	250.00	900.00
753,572	1892	175.00	225.00	350.00
82,968	1892 CC	200.00	250.00	1000.00
10,000	1892 O	450.00	700.00	3500.00
298,400	1892 S	175.00	215.00	650.00
1,528,197	1893	150.00	175.00	275.00
60,000	1893 CC	225.00	315.00	1250.00
110,000	1893 O	215.00	280.00	1000.00
224,000	1893 S	175.00	200.00	650.00
957,955	1894	175.00	200.00	425.00
16,600	1894 O	200.00	300.00	1100.00

QUANTITY	YEAR	FINE	VERY FINE	UNC.
55,900	1894 S	185.00	250.00	1000.00
1,345,936	1895	150.00	175.00	275.00
112,000	1895 S	185.00	215.00	850.00
59,063	1896	175.00	210.00	500.00
155,400	1896 S	175.00	200.00	625.00
867,883	1897	150.00	175.00	275.00
354,000	1897 S	150.00	175.00	500.00
633,495	1898	150.00	175.00	275.00
1,397,400	1898 S	150.00	175.00	275.00
1,710,729	1899	150.00	175.00	275.00
1,545,000	1899 S	150.00	175.00	275.00
1,405,730	1900	150.00	175.00	275.00
329,000	1900 S	150.00	175.00	525.00
616,400	1901	150.00	175.00	275.00
3,648,000	1901 S	150.00	175.00	275.00
172,562	1902	150.00	175.00	275.00
939,000	1902 S	150.00	175.00	275.00
227,024	1903	150.00	175.00	275.00
1,855,000	1903 S	150.00	175.00	275.00
392,136	1904	150.00	175.00	275.00
97,000	1904 S	190.00	215.00	625.00
302,308	1905	150.00	175.00	275.00
880,700	1905 S	150.00	175.00	500.00
348,820	1906	150.00	175.00	275.00
320,000	1906 D	150.00	175.00	275.00
598,000	1906 S	150.00	175.00	275.00
626,192	1907	150.00	175.00	275.00
888,000	1907 D	150.00	175.00	275.00
421,874	1908	150.00	175.00	275.00

INDIAN HEAD INCUSE TYPE

The mint mark is to the left of the eagle's claw on the reverse.

578,012	1908	$175.00	$200.00	$500.00
148,000	1908 D	175.00	200.00	500.00
82,000	1908 S	275.00	500.00	2750.00
627,138	1909	200.00	250.00	750.00
3,423,560	1909 D	175.00	225.00	700.00
34,200	1909 O rare	450.00	725.00	7000.00
297,200	1909 S	225.00	265.00	1500.00
604,250	1910	200.00	250.00	700.00
193,600	1910 D	200.00	250.00	625.00
770,200	1910 S	200.00	250.00	1500.00
915,139	1911	200.00	250.00	500.00
72,500	1911 D	300.00	400.00	4250.00
1,416,000	1911 S	200.00	250.00	900.00
790,144	1912	200.00	250.00	625.00
392,000	1912 S	200.00	275.00	1850.00
916,099	1913	200.00	215.00	550.00
408,000	1913 S	225.00	250.00	2600.00
247,125	1914	200.00	250.00	525.00
247,000	1914 D	200.00	250.00	525.00
263,000	1914 S	200.00	250.00	1250.00
588,075	1915	200.00	200.00	525.00
164,000	1915 S	215.00	225.00	2350.00

QUANTITY	YEAR	FINE	VERY FINE	UNC.
240,000	1916 S	225.00	250.00	825.00
662,000	1929 rare	2000.00	2750.00	6500.00

Eagles ($10)

No value appeared on these coins until 1838.

The eagles and double eagles first issued in 1907 were designed by the distinguished sculptor, Augustus Saint-Gaudens. They are generally considered the most beautiful of all United States coins. Theodore Roosevelt, who was President at the time, forbade the use of the motto "In God We Trust" on these coins. He felt that the appearance of this phrase on a coin was in bad taste. His successor, President Taft, had the motto restored in 1908.

BUST TYPE

1795–1797   **1797–1804**

Eagles ($10 Gold Pieces)

QUANTITY	YEAR	FINE	VERY FINE	UNC.
5,583	1795	$5500.00	$7500.00	$32,500.00
4,146	1796	5250.00	7250.00	35,000.00
14,555	1797 small eagle	4250.00	6750.00	37,500.00
	1797 large eagle	3000.00	5000.00	17,500.00
1,742	1798 over 97; 4 stars before bust	4500.00	7500.00	32,500.00
	1798 over 97; 6 stars before bust	10,000.00	22,500.00	62,500.00
37,449	1799	2000.00	3250.00	12,500.00
5,999	1800	2750.00	3500.00	14,000.00
44,344	1801	2250.00	3250.00	12,000.00
15,017	1803	2250.00	3250.00	13,500.00
3,757	1804	3000.00	5000.00	26,500.00

CORONET TYPE

1838–1865   **1866–1907**

The mint mark is below the eagle on the reverse.

QUANTITY	YEAR	VERY FINE	EXT. FINE	UNC.
7,200	1838	1300.00	2500.00	12,500.00
38,248	1839	900.00	1750.00	9500.00
47,338	1840	425.00	625.00	6750.00
63,131	1841	325.00	500.00	6500.00
2,500	1841 O	1000.00	2500.00	17,500.00
81,507	1842	325.00	625.00	6750.00
27,400	1842 O	375.00	650.00	10,000.00
75,462	1843	350.00	600.00	8250.00
175,162	1843 O	315.00	500.00	5750.00
6,361	1844	575.00	1300.00	8250.00
118,700	1844 O	300.00	500.00	8000.00
26,153	1845	375.00	650.00	8000.00
47,500	1845 O	375.00	650.00	8000.00
20,095	1846	425.00	800.00	8500.00
81,780	1846 O	375.00	525.00	6000.00
862,258	1847	350.00	450.00	3250.00
571,500	1847 O	325.00	450.00	3750.00
145,484	1848	300.00	450.00	4250.00
35,850	1848 O	425.00	750.00	5000.00
653,618	1849	300.00	425.00	3500.00
23,900	1849 O	450.00	725.00	8000.00
291,451	1850	325.00	450.00	3850.00
57,500	1850 O	350.00	625.00	5000.00
176,328	1851	300.00	425.00	4750.00
263,000	1851 O	300.00	425.00	5000.00
263,106	1852	300.00	425.00	4750.00
18,000	1852 O	525.00	1000.00	7500.00
201,253	1853	300.00	450.00	3500.00
51,000	1853 O	325.00	525.00	5500.00
54,250	1854	325.00	525.00	3850.00
52,500	1854 O	325.00	525.00	4250.00
123,826	1854 S	300.00	500.00	4000.00
121,701	1855	285.00	425.00	3500.00
18,000	1855 O	500.00	900.00	6500.00
9,000	1855 S	1000.00	1400.00	10,000.00
60,490	1856	300.00	450.00	3250.00
14,500	1856 O	500.00	1000.00	7500.00
68,000	1856 S	400.00	600.00	6500.00
16,606	1857	375.00	650.00	6750.00
5,500	1857 O	875.00	1650.00	10,000.00
26,000	1857 S	425.00	725.00	6250.00
2,521	1858 ext. rare	4750.00	8750.00	37,500.00
20,000	1858 O	350.00	650.00	7250.00
11,800	1858 S	625.00	1000.00	7500.00
16,093	1859	375.00	750.00	7250.00
2,300	1859 O	1650.00	6250.00	17,500.00
7,000	1859 S	1000.00	1750.00	10,000.00
11,783	1860	365.00	750.00	6750.00
11,100	1860 O	425.00	1000.00	10,000.00
5,000	1860 S	1100.00	1750.00	17,500.00
113,233	1861	285.00	400.00	3750.00
15,500	1861 S	425.00	1200.00	9250.00
10,995	1862	425.00	750.00	5500.00
12,500	1862 S	500.00	1250.00	12,500.00
1,248	1863	3250.00	6250.00	22,500.00
10,000	1863 S	825.00	1250.00	10,000.00
3,580	1864	1000.00	2500.00	12,500.00
2,500	1864 S	2650.00	7500.00	25,000.00
4,005	1865	1000.00	2750.00	12,500.00
16,700	1865 S	1000.00	2500.00	13,500.00
20,000*	1866 S	1350.00	3250.00	14,500.00

CORONET TYPE WITH MOTTO
The mint mark is below the eagle on the reverse.

QUANTITY	YEAR	VERY FINE	EXT. FINE	UNC.
3,780	1866	$625.00	$1250.00	$7500.00
*	1866 S	600.00	1100.00	6250.00

*Includes 1866 S coins with motto.

CORONET TYPE

QUANTITY	YEAR	VERY FINE	EXT. FINE	UNC.
3,140	1867	$1000.00	$1650.00	$9500.00
9,000	1867 S	750.00	1250.00	6500.00
10,655	1868	625.00	900.00	5250.00
13,500	1868 S	625.00	900.00	5250.00
1,855	1869	1000.00	2500.00	10,000.00
6,430	1869 S	1000.00	1500.00	7500.00
2,535	1870	825.00	1250.00	6250.00
5,908	1870 CC	1750.00	8750.00	17,500.00
8,000	1870 S	750.00	1250.00	7250.00
1,780	1871	1600.00	2250.00	8250.00
7,185	1871 CC	875.00	1750.00	6500.00
16,500	1871 S	650.00	850.00	5750.00
1,650	1872	1500.00	2500.00	7500.00
5,500	1872 CC	1000.00	1500.00	7250.00
17,300	1872 S	575.00	1000.00	4750.00
825	1873	3250.00	5000.00	17,500.00
4,543	1873 CC	1250.00	4250.00	12,500.00
12,000	1873 S	625.00	1100.00	6750.00
53,160	1874	300.00	450.00	1250.00
16,767	1874 CC	700.00	1250.00	7250.00
10,000	1874 S	650.00	1000.00	6250.00
120	1875	rare $115,000, Akers Aug. 1990 Auction, Proof		
7,715	1875 CC	825.00	1850.00	8250.00
732	1876	2000.00	6250.00	12,500.00
4,696	1876 CC	1250.00	2000.00	10,000.00
5,000	1876 S	875.00	1750.00	6750.00
817	1877	1250.00	4750.00	17,500.00
3,332	1877 CC	1100.00	3250.00	12,500.00
17,000	1877 S	525.00	825.00	5000.00
73,800	1878	300.00	425.00	1300.00
3,244	1878 CC	1250.00	2500.00	11,000.00
26,100	1878 S	400.00	750.00	3500.00
384,770	1879	275.00	325.00	675.00
1,762	1879 CC	2750.00	6250.00	17,500.00
1,500	1879 O	1750.00	3250.00	14,000.00
224,000	1879 S	265.00	375.00	825.00
1,644,876	1880	250.00	350.00	500.00
11,190	1880 CC	350.00	700.00	2250.00
9,200	1880 O	375.00	725.00	2500.00
506,250	1880 S	275.00	325.00	600.00

CORONET TYPE WITHOUT MOTTO

QUANTITY	YEAR	VERY FINE	EXT. FINE	UNC.
3,877,260	1881	$200.00	$235.00	$300.00
24,015	1881 CC	325.00	450.00	2250.00
8,350	1881 O	375.00	600.00	2850.00
970,000	1881 S	200.00	250.00	300.00
2,324,480	1882	200.00	250.00	285.00
6,764	1882 CC	425.00	875.00	4250.00
10,820	1882 O	350.00	625.00	2750.00
132,000	1882 S	275.00	350.00	750.00
208,740	1883	275.00	350.00	450.00
12,000	1883 CC	375.00	675.00	2850.00
800	1883 O rare	2500.00	4250.00	16,500.00
38,000	1883 S	325.00	400.00	800.00
76,905	1884	325.00	375.00	650.00
9,925	1884 CC	450.00	750.00	4750.00
124,250	1884 S	275.00	350.00	800.00
253,527	1885	275.00	325.00	525.00
228,000	1885 S	275.00	325.00	500.00
236,160	1886	300.00	325.00	500.00
826,000	1886 S	300.00	325.00	450.00
53,680	1887	350.00	375.00	750.00
817,000	1887 S	300.00	325.00	400.00
132,996	1888	300.00	325.00	675.00
21,335	1888 O	300.00	350.00	725.00

QUANTITY	YEAR	VERY FINE	EXT. FINE	UNC.
648,700	1888 S	225.00	325.00	425.00
4,485	1889	400.00	600.00	1650.00
425,400	1889 S	250.00	325.00	415.00
58,043	1890	285.00	350.00	825.00
17,500	1890 CC	350.00	415.00	1200.00
91,868	1891	275.00	340.00	500.00
103,732	1891 CC	275.00	400.00	750.00
797,552	1892	215.00	300.00	400.00
40,000	1892 CC	300.00	450.00	1200.00
28,688	1892 O	265.00	325.00	550.00
115,500	1892 S	250.00	300.00	525.00
1,840,895	1893	225.00	275.00	400.00
14,000	1893 CC	350.00	500.00	2000.00
17,000	1893 O	285.00	340.00	725.00
141,350	1893 S	275.00	320.00	550.00
2,470,778	1894	225.00	275.00	375.00
107,500	1894 O	285.00	315.00	800.00
25,000	1894 S	350.00	425.00	1250.00
567,826	1895	215.00	250.00	375.00
98,000	1895 O	285.00	325.00	525.00
49,00	1895 S	300.00	375.00	1650.00
76,348	1896	250.00	325.00	425.00
123,750	1896 S	285.00	350.00	1250.00
1,000,159	1897	200.00	275.00	350.00
42,500	1897 O	275.00	325.00	700.00
234,750	1897 S	265.00	320.00	750.00
812,197	1898	215.00	300.00	375.00
473,600	1898 S	250.00	320.00	575.00
1,262,305	1899	215.00	300.00	375.00
37,047	1899 O	285.00	340.00	750.00
841,000	1899 S	265.00	320.00	450.00
293,960	1900	250.00	320.00	400.00
81,000	1900 S	265.00	350.00	750.00
1,718,825	1901	215.00	300.00	400.00
72,041	1901 O	285.00	340.00	550.00
2,812,750	1901 S	215.00	300.00	375.00
82,513	1902	225.00	325.00	450.00
469,500	1902 S	215.00	300.00	375.00
125,926	1903	215.00	300.00	375.00
112,771	1903 O	265.00	300.00	450.00
538,000	1903 S	215.00	300.00	400.00
162,038	1904	215.00	300.00	375.00
108,950	1904 O	300.00	350.00	500.00
201,087	1905	250.00	300.00	375.00
369,250	1905 S	275.00	320.00	800.00
165,497	1906	285.00	320.00	425.00
981,000	1906 D	200.00	300.00	375.00
86,895	1906 O	285.00	350.00	550.00
457,000	1906 S	275.00	325.00	600.00
1,203,973	1907	200.00	275.00	375.00
1,030,000	1907 D	200.00	275.00	375.00
210,500	1907 S	320.00	365.00	825.00

INDIAN HEAD TYPE

Without Motto　　　　　**With Motto**

The mint mark is to the left of the eagle's claw on the reverse.

EAGLES: INDIAN HEAD TYPE MOTTO (continued)

QUANTITY	YEAR	VERY FINE	EXT. FINE	UNC.
500	1907 Periods before and after legends. Wire edge			20,000.00
42	1907 As above, but with rolled edge			35,000.00
239,406	1907 No periods	400.00	450.00	1000.00
33,500	1908 No motto	425.00	650.00	1250.00
210,000	1908 D No motto	400.00	500.00	1000.00
341,486	1908 Motto	400.00	425.00	850.00
836,500	1908 D Motto	400.00	425.00	850.00
59,850	1908 S	450.00	750.00	3250.00
184,863	1909	425.00	450.00	750.00
121,540	1909 D	450.00	500.00	1000.00
292,350	1909 S	425.00	500.00	1100.00
318,704	1910	400.00	475.00	800.00
2,356,640	1910 D	385.00	450.00	700.00
811,000	1910 S	400.00	500.00	1000.00
505,595	1911	425.00	500.00	800.00
30,100	1911 D	525.00	800.00	425.00
51,000	1911 S	475.00	750.00	2000.00
405,083	1912	400.00	475.00	650.00
300,000	1912 S	400.00	500.00	1200.00
442,071	1913	400.00	500.00	725.00
66,000	1913 S	525.00	800.00	5000.00
151,050	1914	400.00	500.00	800.00
343,500	1914 D	400.00	500.00	650.00
208,000	1914 S	425.00	525.00	1000.00
351,075	1915	400.00	500.00	750.00
59,000	1915 S	500.00	575.00	2400.00
138,000	1916 S	425.00	550.00	1250.00
126,500	1920 S	800.00	8000.00	20,000.00
1,014,000	1926	400.00	500.00	700.00
96,000	1930 S	3500.00	5000.00	11,000.00
4,463,000	1932	400.00	500.00	700.00
312,500	1933	rare	25,000.00	100,000.00

Double Eagles ($20)

This denomination, the highest in American coinage, made its appearance when gold became plentiful after the discovery of gold in California.

The rarest double eagle is that of 1849. Only one was issued and it is in the collection of the United States Mint.

CORONET TYPE

Without Motto
1850–1865

With Motto
1866–1907

Double Eagles ($20 Gold Pieces)
The mint mark is below the eagle on the reverse.

QUANTITY	YEAR	VERY FINE	EXT. FINE	UNC.
1,170,261	1850	$550.00	$650.00	$3750.00
141,000	1850 O	650.00	825.00	7500.00
2,087,155	1851	525.00	600.00	2500.00
315,000	1851 O	600.00	825.00	7500.00
2,053,026	1852	550.00	635.00	2500.00
190,000	1852 O	600.00	800.00	6500.00
1,261,326	1853	500.00	600.00	5000.00
71,000	1853 O	650.00	1000.00	10,000.00
757,899	1854	525.00	750.00	5500.00
3,250	1854 O		50,000.00	
141,468	1854 S	600.00	725.00	3750.00
364,666	1855	550.00	1000.00	5250.00
8,000	1855 O	2500.00	5000.00	16,500.00
879,675	1855 S	525.00	600.00	5000.00
329,878	1856	525.00	600.00	4750.00
2,250	1856 O		60,000.00	
1,189,750	1856 S	525.00	600.00	4250.00
439,375	1857	550.00	650.00	5500.00
30,000	1857 O	800.00	1200.00	8250.00
970,500	1857 S	525.00	600.00	3750.00
211,714	1858	525.00	600.00	5750.00
32,250	1858 O	875.00	1650.00	11,000.00
846,710	1858 S	550.00	650.00	5000.00
43,597	1859	800.00	1400.00	12,500.00
9,100	1859 O	2000.00	4250.00	17,500.00
636,445	1859 S	550.00	750.00	5250.00
577,670	1860	550.00	650.00	4250.00
6,600	1860 O	2750.00	4500.00	18,500.00
544,950	1860 S	550.00	700.00	6750.00
2,976,453	1861	550.00	650.00	2500.00
5,000	1861 O	1500.00	3000.00	15,000.00
768,000	1861 S	550.00	650.00	6500.00
?	1861 S Paquet's reverse $660,000.00 Nov. 1988 Norweb Sale			
92,133	1862	750.00	950.00	7500.00
854,173	1862 S	600.00	700.00	6500.00
142,790	1863	600.00	675.00	5500.00
966,570	1863 S	525.00	625.00	4750.00
204,285	1864	600.00	750.00	4500.00
793,660	1864 S	525.00	625.00	4750.00
351,200	1865	600.00	650.00	4500.00
1,042,500	1865 S	575.00	650.00	4650.00
?	1866 S No motto	750.00	1200.00	8750.00
698,775	1866	525.00	625.00	4500.00
842,250	1866 S	525.00	625.00	3850.00
251,065	1867	525.00	625.00	1250.00
920,750	1867 S	525.00	625.00	3750.00
98,000	1868	550.00	650.00	4000.00
837,500	1868 S	525.00	750.00	3750.00
175,155	1869	525.00	650.00	4650.00
686,750	1869 S	525.00	625.00	3850.00
155,185	1870	525.00	650.00	3850.00
3,789	1870 CC		45,000.00	
982,000	1870 S	525.00	625.00	3750.00
80,150	1871	550.00	650.00	4000.00
14,687	1871 CC	1850.00	3500.00	17,500.00
928,000	1871 S	525.00	625.00	3750.00
251,880	1872	550.00	650.00	2500.00
29,650	1872 CC	750.00	1500.00	8500.00
780,000	1872 S	525.00	625.00	2000.00
1,709,825	1873	525.00	625.00	900.00
22,410	1873 CC	750.00	1250.00	8500.00
1,040,600	1873 S	525.00	625.00	1300.00
366,800	1874	525.00	625.00	1400.00
115,085	1874 CC	625.00	875.00	6500.00
1,214,000	1874 S	525.00	650.00	1200.00
295,740	1875	525.00	625.00	1000.00
111,151	1875 CC	600.00	750.00	2000.00
1,230,000	1875 S	525.00	625.00	900.00

DOUBLE EAGLES: CORONET TYPE (continued)

QUANTITY	YEAR	VERY FINE	EXT. FINE	UNC.
583,905	1876	525.00	625.00	900.00
138,441	1876 CC	625.00	750.00	3250.00
1,597,000	1876 S	525.00	625.00	1000.00
397,670	1877	525.00	625.00	850.00
42,565	1877 CC	650.00	850.00	6250.00
1,735,000	1877 S	525.00	625.00	800.00
543,645	1878	525.00	625.00	750.00
13,180	1878 CC	775.00	1200.00	7500.00
1,739,000	1878 S	525.00	625.00	800.00
207,630	1879	525.00	625.00	1000.00
10,708	1879 CC	900.00	1800.00	9500.00
2,325	1879 O	2600.00	4500.00	18,500.00
1,223,800	1879 S	525.00	625.00	800.00
51,456	1880	525.00	650.00	1750.00
836,000	1880 S	525.00	625.00	1500.00
2,260	1881	3500.00	8500.00	20,000.00
727,000	1881 S	475.00	550.00	1250.00
630	1882 rare	5000.00	8500.00	37,500.00
39,140	1882 CC	675.00	850.00	4750.00
1,125,000	1882 S	525.00	625.00	1000.00
40	1883 very rare (only proofs were struck)			95,000.00
59,962	1883 CC	650.00	850.00	3750.00
1,189,000	1883 S	475.00	550.00	650.00
71	1884 very rare (only proofs)			$71,500.00
	Stack's Nov. 1989 Sale			
81,139	1884 CC	675.00	850.00	2850.00
916,000	1884 S	425.00	500.00	600.00
828	1885	5000.00	8500.00	27,500.00
9,450	1885 CC	1100.00	1750.00	7500.00
683,500	1885 S	525.00	625.00	700.00
1,106	1886	6000.00	12,000.00	27,500.00
121	1887 rare (only proofs were struck)			42,500.00
283,000	1887 S	425.00	500.00	750.00
226,266	1888	425.00	500.00	700.00
859,600	1888 S	425.00	500.00	650.00
44,111	1889	525.00	675.00	900.00
30,945	1889 CC	625.00	800.00	3250.00
774,700	1889 S	500.00	625.00	750.00
75,995	1890	500.00	625.00	800.00
91,209	1890 CC	625.00	775.00	3250.00
802,750	1890 S	500.00	625.00	850.00
1,442	1891	2400.00	3750.00	12,500.00
5,000	1891 CC	1850.00	2750.00	10,000.00
1,288,125	1891 S	475.00	550.00	600.00
4,523	1892	1000.00	1500.00	5250.00
27,265	1892 CC	650.00	1200.00	3750.00
930,150	1892 S	475.00	550.00	600.00
344,339	1893	475.00	550.00	600.00
18,402	1893 CC	675.00	900.00	2750.00
996,175	1893 S	475.00	550.00	600.00
1,368,990	1894	425.00	500.00	550.00
1,048,550	1894 S	425.00	500.00	550.00
1,114,656	1895	425.00	500.00	550.00
1,143,500	1895 S	425.00	500.00	550.00
792,663	1896	450.00	525.00	575.00
1,403,925	1896 S	425.00	525.00	550.00
1,383,261	1897	425.00	525.00	550.00
1,470,250	1897 S	425.00	525.00	550.00
170,470	1898	475.00	575.00	750.00
2,575,175	1898 S	425.00	525.00	550.00
1,669,384	1899	425.00	525.00	550.00
2,010,300	1899 S	425.00	525.00	550.00
1,874,584	1900	425.00	525.00	550.00
2,459,500	1900 S	425.00	525.00	550.00
111,526	1901	475.00	550.00	700.00
1,596,000	1901 S	425.00	550.00	625.00

QUANTITY	YEAR	VERY FINE	EXT. FINE	UNC.
31,254	1902	600.00	675.00	850.00
1,753,625	1902 S	450.00	525.00	600.00
287,428	1903	500.00	600.00	700.00
954,000	1903 S	450.00	550.00	600.00
6,256,797	1904	425.00	550.00	600.00
5,134,175	1904 S	425.00	550.00	600.00
59,011	1905	500.00	600.00	1100.00
1,813,000	1905 S	450.00	525.00	600.00
69,600	1906	500.00	600.00	850.00
620,250	1906 D	425.00	500.00	600.00
2,065,750	1906 S	425.00	500.00	600.00
1,451,864	1907	425.00	500.00	600.00
842,250	1907 D	450.00	600.00	700.00
2,165,800	1907 S	450.00	500.00	600.00

LIBERTY STANDING (SAINT-GAUDENS) TYPE

Without Motto
1907–1908

With Motto
1908–1933

The mint mark is above the date on the reverse.

16	* 1907 very high relief (ext. rare)		$400,000.00	
11,250	1907 MCMVII date high relief			
	with wire edge	$3500.00	$4500.00	$10,000.00
	1907 same			
	with flat edge	4000.00	5000.00	11,000.00
361,667	1907 Arabic date	525.00	600.00	700.00
4,271,551	1908 no motto	500.00	575.00	650.00
663,750	1908 D no motto	500.00	600.00	675.00
156,359	1908 motto	500.00	600.00	675.00
349,500	1908 D motto	500.00	600.00	675.00
22,000	1908 S motto		1100.00	4000.00
161,282	1909 over 8	500.00	700.00	1250.00
	1909	500.00	600.00	700.00
52,500	1909 D	600.00	650.00	1750.00
2,774,925	1909 S	500.00	575.00	675.00
482,167	1910	525.00	600.00	700.00
429,000	1910 D	525.00	600.00	700.00
2,128,250	1910 S	525.00	600.00	700.00
197,350	1911	525.00	600.00	700.00
846,500	1911 D	525.00	600.00	700.00
775,750	1911 S	525.00	600.00	700.00
149,824	1912	550.00	625.00	725.00
168,838	1913	500.00	600.00	700.00
393,500	1913 D	500.00	600.00	700.00
34,000	1913 S	550.00	650.00	1100.00
95,320	1914	525.00	625.00	725.00
453,000	1914 D	500.00	575.00	700.00
1,498,000	1914 S	500.00	575.00	700.00
152,050	1915	525.00	650.00	725.00
567,500	1915 S	500.00	600.00	700.00

DOUBLE EAGLES: LIBERTY STANDING (SAINT-GAUDENS) TYPE (continued)

QUANTITY	YEAR	VERY FINE	EXT. FINE	UNC.
796,000	1916 S	500.00	600.00	675.00
228,250	1920	500.00	600.00	675.00
558,000	1920 S	4500.00	10,000.00	16,500.00
528,500	1921	7000.00	12,500.00	30,000.00
1,375,500	1922	500.00	600.00	675.00
2,658,000	1922 S	550.00	600.00	1000.00
566,000	1923	525.00	600.00	700.00
1,702,000	1923 D	500.00	600.00	675.00
4,323,500	1924	500.00	600.00	700.00
3,049,500	1924 D	700.00	800.00	1850.00
2,927,500	1924 S	750.00	900.00	1800.00
2,831,750	1925	500.00	600.00	700.00
2,938,500	1925 D	800.00	1000.00	3200.00
3,776,500	1925 S	750.00	850.00	2000.00
816,750	1926	600.00	700.00	800.00
481,000	1926 D	900.00	1250.00	2750.00
2,041,500	1926 S	750.00	900.00	2000.00
2,946,750	1927	525.00	600.00	675.00
180,000	1927 D $522,500 Stacks March 1991 Sale, MS-65			
3,107,000	1927 S	2000.00	4000.00	11,000.00
8,816,000	1928	500.00	550.00	650.00
1,779,750	1929	3000.00	4500.00	11,000.00
74,000	1930 S		10,000.00	25,000.00
2,938,250	1931		8500.00	18,500.00
106,500	1931 D		10,000.00	20,000.00
1,101,750	1932		9000.00	19,000.00
445,500	1933 not officially released			

*The very high relief experimental pieces show 14 rays extending from the sun on the reverse side. The regular issue high relief coins have only 13 rays.

BULLION COINS

The United States struck its first gold bullion coin, the American Eagle, on September 8, 1986 at the West Point, NY Bullion Depository. The American Eagle is being issued in four sizes with nominal dollar values inscribed upon them. The $50 denomination contains 1 troy ounce of bullion, while the 1/2, 1/4, and 1/10 ounce sizes are denominated at $25, $10, and $5, respectively. All coins will be sold at prices according to prevailing market quotations for bullion. The appearance of the $50 bullion coin in particular has resulted in a declining collector interest in the St. Gaudens $20 gold piece of 1907–33 since the designs are so similar.

1986 U.S. $50 gold bullion coin

The U.S. also issued its first silver bullion coin in 1986, the "Silver Eagle," denominated at $1. It contains one troy ounce of silver. The obverse features Adolph A. Weinman's "Walking Liberty" design used on the half-dollar coins from 1916 to 1947, while the reverse design is a rendition of a heraldic eagle by John Mercanti, a Mint sculptor and engraver.

1986 U.S. $1 silver bullion coin

COMMEMORATIVE COINS

American commemorative coins make up the handsomest and most varied series in all our coinage. Almost all buying and selling of these coins are in the uncirculated state; the commemoratives have never been intended for general use. To date there are over 100 major varieties of silver commemorative coins and some 50 gold commemorative coins.

Several of these coins have been issued in a considerable variety of dates and mint marks. The Texas Centennial coin, for example, has 13 such varieties. For the collector who is not a specialist, the advisable course is to limit himself to the cheapest variety of such a coin. In this way he will be able to acquire the largest number of commemorative coins.

The gold commemorative coins are of course more expensive than the silver coins which make up the bulk of the commemorative coinage. The two outstanding rarities among commemorative coins are the 1915 S Panama-Pacific $50 gold pieces.

SILVER COMMEMORATIVE COINS
(Half Dollars unless otherwise specified)

QUANTITY	YEAR	UNC.
950,000	1892 Columbian Exposition	$65.00
1,550,405	1893 Columbian Exposition	60.00
24,191	1893 Isabella Quarter	550.00
36,000	1900 Lafayette Dollar	1200.00
27,134	1915 S Panama-Pacific Exposition	400.00
100,058	1918 Illinois Centennial	125.00
50,028	1920 Maine Centennial	150.00
152,112	* 1920 Pilgrim Tercentenary	85.00

1892 Columbian Exposition

SILVER COMMEMORATIVE COINS (continued)

1920 Pilgrim Tercentenary

QUANTITY	YEAR	UNC.
20,053	*1921 Pilgrim Tercentenary (1921 on obverse)	125.00
5,000	1921 Missouri Centennial (2 [mult] 4)	500.00
15,400	1921 Missouri Centennial (no 2 [mult] 4)	450.00
6,006	1921 Alabama Centennial (with 2 [mult] 2)	300.00
49,038	1921 Alabama Centennial (no 2 [mult] 2)	250.00
4,250	1922 Grant Memorial (with star)	825.00
67,411	1922 Grant Memorial (no star)	125.00
274,077	1923 S Monroe Doctrine Centennial	75.00
142,080	1924 Huguenot-Walloon Tercentenary	125.00
162,099	1925 Lexington-Concord Sesquicentennial	80.00
1,314,709	1925 Stone Mountain Memorial	50.00
86,594	1925 S California Diamond Jubilee	175.00
14,994	1925 Fort Vancouver Centennial	400.00
141,120	1926 Sesquicentennial of American Independence	75.00
48,030	1926 Oregon Trail Memorial	125.00
86,354	1926 S Oregon Trail Memorial	125.00
6,028	1928 Oregon Trail Memorial	200.00
5,008	1933 D Oregon Trail Memorial	225.00
7,006	1934 D Oregon Trail Memorial	175.00
10,006	1936 Oregon Trail Memorial	125.00
5,006	1936 S Oregon Trail Memorial	185.00
12,008	1937 D Oregon Trail Memorial	135.00
6,006	1938 Oregon Trail Memorial	
6,005	1938 D Oregon Trail Memorial	
6,006	1938 S Oregon Trail Memorial	
	1938 P-D-S (set of three)	500.00
3,004	1939 Oregon Trail Memorial	
3,004	1939 D Oregon Trail Memorial	
3,005	1939 S Oregon Trail Memorial	
	1939 P-D-S (set of three)	1000.00
28,142	1927 Vermont Sesquicentennial	250.00
10,008	1928 Hawaiian Sesquicentennial	1200.00
25,015	1934 Maryland Tercentenary	175.00
61,350	1934 Texas Centennial	125.00
9,994	1935 Texas Centennial	
10,007	1935 D Texas Centennial	
10,008	1935 S Texas Centennial	
	1935 P-D-S (set of three)	325.00
8,911	1936 Texas Centennial	
9,039	1936 D Texas Centennial	
9,064	1936 S Texas Centennial	
	1936 P-D-S (set of three)	325.00
6,571	1937 Texas Centennial	
6,605	1937 D Texas Centennial	
6,637	1937 S Texas Centennial	
	1937 P-D-S (set of three)	425.00
3,780	1938 Texas Centennial	
3,775	1938 D Texas Centennial	
3,816	1938 S Texas Centennial	
	1938 P-D-S (set of three)	650.00
10,007	1934 Daniel Boone Bicentennial	125.00
10,010	1935 Daniel Boone Bicentennial	
5,005	1935 D Daniel Boone Bicentennial	
5,005	1935 S Daniel Boone Bicentennial	
	1935 P-D-S (set of three)	325.00
10,008	*1935 Daniel Boone Bicentennial	
2,003	*1935 D Daniel Boone Bicentennial	
2,004	*1935 S Daniel Boone Bicentennial	
	1935 P-D-S (set of three)	875.00
12,012	1936 Daniel Boone Bicentennial	
5,005	1936 D Daniel Boone Bicentennial	
5,006	1936 S Daniel Boone Bicentennial	
	1936 P-D-S (set of three)	325.00

Oregon Trail Memorial

Texas Centennial

*Of the total 1920–1921 issue, 148,000 coins were melted down by the Mint.

QUANTITY	YEAR	UNC.
9,810	1937 Daniel Boone Bicentennial	
2,506	1937 D Daniel Boone Bicentennial	
2,506	1937 S Daniel Boone Bicentennial	
	1937 P-D-S (set of three)	650.00
2,100	1938 Daniel Boone Bicentennial	
2,100	1938 D Daniel Boone Bicentennial	
2,100	1938 S Daniel Boone Bicentennial	
	1938 P-D-S (set of three)	1200.00
25,018	1935 Connecticut Tercentenary	225.00
13,012	1935 Arkansas Centennial	100.00
5,505	1935 D Arkansas Centennial	100.00
5,506	1935 S Arkansas Centennial	100.00
9,660	1936 Arkansas Centennial	
9,660	1936 D Arkansas Centennial	
9,662	1936 S Arkansas Centennial	
	1936 P-D-S (set of three)	300.00
5,505	1937 Arkansas Centennial	
5,505	1937 D Arkansas Centennial	
5,506	1937 S Arkansas Centennial	
	1937 P-D-S (set of three)	400.00
3,156	1938 Arkansas Centennial	
3,155	1938 D Arkansas Centennial	
3,156	1938 S Arkansas Centennial	
	1938 P-D-S (set of three)	550.00
2,104	1939 Arkansas Centennial	
2,104	1939 D Arkansas Centennial	
2,105	1939 S Arkansas Centennial	
	1939 P-D-S (set of three)	1100.00
10,008	1935 Hudson, N. Y. Sesquicentennial	700.00
70,132	1935 S California-Pacific Exposition	100.00
30,092	1936 D California-Pacific Exposition	135.00
10,008	1935 Old Spanish Trail	850.00
20,013	1936 Rhode Island Tercentenary	
15,010	1936 D Rhode Island Tercentenary	
15,011	1936 S Rhode Island Tercentenary	
	1936 P-D-S (set of three)	325.00
50,030	1936 Cleveland, Great Lakes Exposition	125.00
25,015	1936 Wisconsin Territorial Centennial	250.00
5,005	1936 Cincinnati Musical Center	
5,005	1936 D Cincinnati Musical Center	
5,006	1936 S Cincinnati Musical Center	
	1936 P-D-S (set of three)	1000.00
81,773	1936 Long Island Tercentenary	125.00
25,015	1936 York County, Maine Tercentenary	250.00
25,015	1936 Bridgeport, Conn. Centennial	200.00
20,013	1936 Lynchburg, Va. Sesquicentennial	250.00
20,015	1936 Elgin, Illinois Centennial	275.00
16,687	1936 Albany, N. Y. Charter	325.00
71,369	1936 S San Francisco-Oakland Bay Bridge	135.00
9,007	1936 Columbia, S. C. Sesquicentennial	
8,009	1936 D Columbia, S. C. Sesquicentennial	
8,007	1936 S Columbia, S. C. Sesquicentennial	
	1936 P-D-S (set of three)	750.00
25,265	1936 Arkansas Centennial-Robinson	125.00
25,015	1936 Delaware Tercentenary	275.00
26,928	1936 Battle of Gettysburg (1863–1938)	300.00
15,000	1936 Norfolk, Va. Bicentennial	500.00
29,030	1937 Roanoke Island, N. C. (1587–1937)	250.00
18,028	1937 Battle of Antietam (1862–1937)	500.00
15,266	1938 New Rochelle, N. Y. (1688–1938)	500.00
100,057	1946 Iowa Centennial	125.00
1,000,546	1946 Booker T. Washington Memorial	12.50
200,113	1946 D Booker T. Washington Memorial	15.00
500,279	1946 S Booker T. Washington Memorial	12.50
	1946 P-D-S (set of three)	50.00
100,017	1947 Booker T. Washington Memorial	

**Daniel Boone
Bicentennial**

Arkansas Centennial

Old Spanish Trail

**San Francisco-Oakland
Bay Bridge**

*Small "1934" added on reverse.

SILVER COMMEMORATIVE (continued)

**Booker T. Washington
Memorial**

Carver-Washington

QUANTITY	YEAR	UNC.
100,017	1947 D Booker T. Washington Memorial	
100,017	1947 S Booker T. Washington Memorial 1	
	947 P-D-S (set of three)	65.00
8,005	1948 Booker T. Washington Memorial	
8,005	1948 D Booker T. Washington Memorial	
8,005	1948 S Booker T. Washington Memorial	
	1948 P-D-S (set of three)	130.00
6,004	1949 Booker T. Washington Memorial	
6,004	1949 D Booker T. Washington Memorial	
6,004	1949 S Booker T. Washington Memorial	
	1949 P-D-S (set of three)	200.00
6,004	1950 Booker T. Washington Memorial	
6,004	1950 D Booker T. Washington Memorial	
512,091	1950 S Booker T. Washington Memorial	
	1950 P-D-S (set of three)	160.00
510,082	1951 Booker T. Washington Memorial	
12,004	1951 D Booker T. Washington Memorial	
12,004	1951 S Booker T. Washington Memorial	
	1951 P-D-S (set of three)	110.00
110,018	1951 Carver-Washington	12.50
10,004	1951 D Carver-Washington	
10,004	1951 S Carver-Washington	
	1951 P-D-S (set of three)	100.00
2,006,292	1952 Carver-Washington	12.50
6,003	1952 D Carver-Washington	
6,003	1952 S Carver-Washington	
	1952 P-D-S (set of three)	115.00
8,003	1953 Carver-Washington	
8,003	1953 D Carver-Washington	
108,020	1953 S Carver-Washington	
	1953 P-D-S (set of three)	165.00
12,006	1954 Carver-Washington	
12,006	1954 D Carver-Washington	
122,024	1954 S Carver-Washington	
	1954 P-D-S (set of three)	90.00
2,210,502	1982 D George Washington	
	(250th anniversary of birth)	12.50
4,894,044	1982 S George Washington (proof)	15.00

GOLD COMMEMORATIVE COINS
(Dollars unless otherwise specified)

**1915 S Panama-Pacific
Exposition**

QUANTITY	YEAR	UNC.
17,375	1903 Louisiana Purchase (Jefferson)	$800.00
17,375	1903 Louisiana Purchase (McKinley)	800.00
9,997	1904 Lewis and Clark Exposition	1250.00
10,000	1905 Lewis and Clark Exposition	1500.00
25,000	1915 S Panama-Pacific Exposition	1000.00
6,749	1915 S Panama-Pacific Exposition	
	($2.50)	2500.00
483	1915 S Panama-Pacific Exposition	
	($50 round)	45,000.00
645	1915 S Panama-Pacific Exposition	
	($50 octagonal)	30,000.00
9,977	1916 McKinley Memorial	875.00
10,000	1917 McKinley Memorial	825.00
5,000	1922 Grant Memorial (with star)	1750.00
5,000	1922 Grant Memorial (no star)	1750.00
46,019	1926 Philadelphia	
	Sesquicentennial ($2.50)	675.00

1984 LOS ANGELES OLYMPICS COMMEMORATIVE COIN SET

One Dollar Silver

QUANTITY	YEAR	BU-65
920,485	1983 Ancient Greek Discus Thrower	$35.00
597,157	1983 D Same Type	40.00
662,837	1983 S Same Type	40.00
4,575,837	1983 S Same Type (proof)	35.00
470,131	1984 Olympic Coliseum Dollar	35.00
316,778	1984 D Same Type	40.00
339,970	1984 S Same Type	40.00
2,623,609	1984 S Same Type (proof)	35.00

Ten Dollars Gold

QUANTITY	YEAR	BU-65
40,000	1984 Two Runners Bearing Olympic Torch Aloft	$385.00
44,000	1984 D Same Type	385.00
55,000	1984 S Same Type	385.00
100,000	1984 W (West Point Mint) Same Type	385.00
661,000	1984 W (proof)	385.00

STATUE OF LIBERTY CENTENNIAL SET

50 Cents Clad

QUANTITY	YEAR	MS-65	PROOF-65
928,008	1986 D	$7.50	—
6,925,627	1986 S (Proof)	—	12.50

One Dollar Silver

723,635	1986 P	27.50	—
6,414,638	1986 S (Proof)	—	35.00

Five Dollars Gold

95,248	1986 W (West Point)	250.00	—
404,013	1986 W (Proof)	—	200.00

Statue of Liberty

CONSTITUTIONAL BICENTENNIAL

One Dollar Silver

451,629	1987 P	$35.00	—
2,747,116	1987 S (Proof)	—	40.00

Five Dollars Gold

214,225	1987 W	250.00	—
651,659	1987 W (Proof)	—	200.00

1988 SEOUL, KOREA OLYMPICS COMMEMORATIVE COIN SET

One Dollar Silver

QUANTITY	YEAR	MS-65	PROOF-65
191,368	1988 D	$25.00	—
1,359,366	1988 S (Proof)	—	30.00

Five Dollars Gold

	YEAR	MS-65	UNC.
62,913	1988 W	225.00	—
281,465	1988 W (Proof)	—	200.00

U.S. CONGRESS BICENTENNIAL SET

50 Cents Clad

163,753	1989 D	$7.50	—
767,897	1989 S (Proof)	—	10.00

One Dollar Silver

135,203	1989 D	25.00	—
762,198	1989 S (Proof)	—	30.00

U.S. Congress Bicentennial Set

		Five Dollars Gold	
QUANTITY	YEAR	MS-65	PROOF-65
46,899	1989 W	200.00	—
281,456	1989 W (Proof)	—	225.00

DWIGHT D. EISENHOWER CENTENNIAL SILVER DOLLAR

Dwight D. Eisenhower Centennial

QUANTITY	YEAR	MS-65	PROOF-65
241,669	1990 W	$27.50	—
1,144,461	1990 (Proof)	—	35.00

Future Commemorative Issues

U.S. Mint Plans Elaborate Coin Program to Commemorate the 26th International Summer Olympic Games Scheduled for Atlanta in 1996.

As this book goes to press, the United States Mint is in the midst of elaborate preparations to strike an ambitious set of coins to commemorate the 26th International Summer Olympic Games scheduled for Atlanta, an affair that will mark the centennial of the modern Olympic Games.

At the moment, plans are to mint two $5 gold coins in each of 1995 and 1996, four silver dollars in 1995–96, and two clad (copper-nickel) half-dollars in each of those two years as well.

Since each of those 16 major varieties of coins is to be produced in both Proof and Uncirculated, there will be 32 types in all, making this the longest commemorative set ever released by the U.S. Mint.

MOUNT RUSHMORE GOLDEN ANNIVERSARY

	Half Dollar Copper-Nickel		
QUANTITY	YEAR	MS-65	PROOF-65
172,754	1991 D	$12.00	—
753,257	1991 S	—	15.00
	One Dollar Silver		
133,139	1991	27.50	—
738,419	1991 S	—	35.00
	Five Dollars Gold		
31,959	1991 W	200.00	225.00

One Dollar Silver

Five Dollars Gold

KOREAN WAR MEMORIAL

QUANTITY	YEAR	One Dollar Silver MS-65	PROOF-65
213,049	1991 D	$22.00	—
618,488	1991 S	—	25.00

USO Golden One Dollar Silver

UNITED SERVICE ORGANIZATIONS GOLDEN ANNIVERSARY

		One Dollar Silver	
124,958	1991 D	$22.00	—
321,275	1991 S	—	25.00

Olympic Half Dollar Clad

1992 BARCELONA SUMMER OLYMPICS COMMEMORATIVE COIN SET

		Half Dollar Clad	
161,619	1992 ("The graceful gymnast")	$8.00	—
519,699	1992 S (Proof)	—	10.00

		One Dollar Silver	
187,562	1992 ("The focused pitcher")	$30.00	—
504,544	1992 S (Proof)	—	32.00

Olympic One Dollar Silver

		Five Dollars Gold	
127,732	1992 W ("The determined sprinter")	$200.00	—
77,313	1992 W (Proof)	—	225.00

Olympic Five Dollars Gold

CHRISTOPHER COLUMBUS QUINCENTENARY COMMEMORATIVE COIN SET

		Half Dollar	
135,718	1992	$12.50	—
390,255	1992 S (Proof)	—	15.00

		Silver Dollar	
106,962	1992	$25.00	—,
385,290	1992 S (Proof)	—	35.00

Columbus Half Dollar

		Five Dollars Gold	
24,331	1992	$225.00	—
79,734	1992 S (Proof)	—	250.00

Columbus One Dollar Silver

Columbus Five Dollars Gold

Proof Sets

In modern times the Mint has issued specially struck proof coins in the cent, nickel, dime, quarter, and half dollar denominations. Premium values are as follows:

YEAR	VALUE	YEAR	VALUE	YEAR	VALUE
1936	$4250.00	1961	17.50	1983 S	15.00
1937	2500.00	1962	17.50	1984 S	15.00
1938	1250.00	1963	17.50	1984 S	
1939	1100.00	1964	15.00	(Olympic dollar)	85.00
1940	850.00	1968 S	8.00	1985 S	12.50
1941	875.00	1969 S	15.00	1986 S	10.00
1942*	900.00	1970 S	12.50	1987 S	10.00
1950	425.00	1971 S	10.00	1988 S	10.00
1951	300.00	1972 S	10.00	1989 S	10.00
1952	150.00	1973 S	12.50	1990 S	22.50
1953	125.00	1974 S	9.00	1991 S	22.50
1954	75.00	1975 S	15.00	1992 S	22.50
1955	75.00	1976 S	15.00	1993 S	25.00
1956	40.00	1977 S	12.00	1994 S	25.00
1957	25.00	1978 S	12.50	1995 S	25.00
1958	30.00	1979 S	12.50		
1959	22.00	1980 S	12.50		
1960 Large date	$20.00	1981 S	12.50		
1960 Small date	35.00	1982 S	10.00		

*Includes both types of nickels issued in 1942.

New U.S. Issues

WHITE HOUSE
BICENTENNIAL COMMEMORATIVE
One Dollar Silver

QUANTITY	YEAR	MS-65	PROOF-65
123,803	1992	$75.00	—
375,849	1992 S (Proof)	—	85.00

One Dollar Silver

BILL OF RIGHTS
COMMEMORATIVE COIN SET
Silver Half Dollar

173,224	1993 W	$17.50	—
559,758	1993 S (Proof)	—	20.00
	One Dollar Silver		
92,415	1993 D	$27.50	—
515,038	1993 S (Proof)	—	27.50
	Five Dollars Gold		
22,897	1993 W	$225.00	—
79,422	1993 P (Proof)	—	225.00

One Dollar Silver

WORLD WAR II 50TH ANNIVERSARY COMMEMORATIVE COIN SET

(The coins are dated 1991–95, but were all struck in 1992.)

Half Dollar Clad

QUANTITY	YEAR	MS-65	PROOF-65
192,968	1993	$10.00	—
290,343	1993 (Proof)	—	12.00

Silver Dollar

94,700	1993 D	25.00	—
515,038	1993 W (Proof)	—	30.00

Five Dollars Gold

23,089	1993 W	180.00	—
65,461	1993 W (Proof)	—	200.00

Clad Half Dollar

THOMAS JEFFERSON, 250TH ANNIVERSARY OF BIRTH

Commemorative Silver Dollar

1993 (1994) (P)	$27.50	—
1993 (1994) S (Proof)	—	32.50

(Note: The Jefferson coins were struck in 1993, but dated 1994.)

Silver Dollar

VIETNAM VETERANS MEMORIAL

One Dollar Silver

1994 W	$27.50	—
1994 P (Proof)	—	32.50

Five Dollars Gold

NATIONAL PRISONER OF WAR MUSEUM

One Dollar Silver

1994 W	$27.50	—
1994 P (Proof)	—	32.50

One Dollar Silver

WOMEN IN MILITARY SERVICE FOR AMERICA MEMORIAL

One Dollar Silver

1994 W	$27.50	—
1994 P (Proof)	—	32.50

1994 WORLD CUP SOCCER TOURNAMENT HELD IN THE UNITED STATES COMMEMORATIVE COIN SET

Clad Half Dollar

1994 W	$10.00	—
1994 (P) (Proof)	—	12.50

Silver Dollar

1994 D	27.50	—
1994 S (Proof)	—	35.00

Five Dollars Gold

1994 W	180.00	—
1994 W (Proof)	—	200.00

One Dollar Silver

One Dollar Silver

UNITED STATES CAPITOL, WASHINGTON, D.C., BICENTENNIAL
Commemorative Silver Dollar

QUANTITY	YEAR	MS-65	PROOF-65
	1994 (P)	$27.50	—
	1994 S (Proof)	—	32.50

U.S. Capitol Silver Dollar

CIVIL WAR BATTLEFIELD COMMEMORATIVE

Half Dollar Clad
(Drummer/Cannon)

1995 S	$10.00	—
1995 S (Proof)	—	12.00

Silver Dollar
(Medical corpsman with soldier/Inscription)

1995 P	30.00	—
1995 S (Proof)	—	35.00

Five Dollars Gold
(Bugler on horseback/U.S. Eagle)

1995 W	200.00	—
1995 W (Proof)	—	225.00

CENTENNIAL OF THE MODERN OLYMPIC GAMES COMMEMORATIVE COIN SET

Since each of the 16 major varieties of coins in the 1996 26th International Summer Olympic Games, set for Atlanta, Georgia, is being produced in both Proof and Uncirculated, there will be 32 types in all, making this the longest commemorative set ever released by the U.S. Mint.

According to the U.S. Mint, the coins were to be released four at a time—one gold, two silver and one clad (eight in all counting the proofs)—in February 1995, July 1995, January 1996 and spring 1996.

Clad Half Dollars

i and ii Clad Half Dollars

i—Baseball

1995 D	$12.50	—
1995 S (Proof)	—	15.00

ii—Basketball

1995 D	12.50	—
1995 S (Proof)	—	15.00

(Note: Common reverse for the two 1995 clad half dollars: a Panoramic Globe.)

Silver Dollars
iii—Gymnastics

1995 D	30.00	—
1995 S (Proof)	—	37.50

iii, iv, v and vi Silver Dollars

QUANTITY	YEAR	MS-65	PROOF-65

iv—Paralympics, Blind Runner
1995 D	$30.00	—
1995 S (Proof)	—	37.50

v—Athletics, Track and Field
1995 D	30.00	—
1995 S (Proof)	—	37.50

vi—Cycling
1995 D	30.00	—
1995 S (Proof)	—	37.50

(Note: Common reverse for all 1995 dollar coins: Clasped Hands.)

Five Dollars Gold

vii—Torch Runner
1995 D	250.00	—
1995 S (Proof)	—	275.00

viii—Olympic Stadium
1995 D	250.00	—
1995 S (Proof)	—	275.00

(Note: Common reverse for the two 1995 gold coins: the American Eagle design by the noted engraver Frank Gasparro.)

Clad Half Dollars

ix—Swimming
1996 D	12.50	—
1996 S (Proof)	—	15.00

x—Soccer
1996 D	12.50	—
1996 S (Proof)	—	15.00

(Note: Common reverse for the two 1996 clad half dollars: "Atlanta Centennial Olympic Games" logo designed by Clint Hansen.)

Silver Dollars

xi—Tennis
1996 D	30.00	—
1996 S (Proof)	—	37.50

xii—Paralympics—Wheelchair Athlete
1996 D	30.00	—
1996 S (Proof)	—	37.50

xiii—Rowing
1996 D	30.00	—
1996 S (Proof)	—	37.50

vii, viii Five Dollars Gold

ix, x Clad Half Dollars

xi, xii, xiii, and xiv Silver Dollars

xv, xvi Five Dollars Gold

OLYMPIC SILVER DOLLARS (continued)

QUANTITY	YEAR	MS-65	PROOF-65

xiv—High Jump

	1996 D	$30.00	—
	1996 S (Proof)	—	37.50

(Note: Common reverse for all 1996 dollar coins: "Atlanta Centennial Olympic Games" logo designed by Thomas D. Rogers.)

Five Dollars Gold

xv—Flag Bearer

	1996 D	250.00	—
	1996 S (Proof)	—	275.00

xv—Flag Bearer

xvi—Cauldron

	1996 D	250.00	—
	1996 S (Proof)	—	275.00

(Note: Common reverse for the two 1996 gold coins: "Atlanta Centennial Olympic Games" logo, with wreath designed by William Krawczewicz.)

3

CATALOG OF
CANADIAN COINS

The coinage of Canada is much less ramified than United States coinage. The Province of Canada had its first coinage in 1858, and the Dominion's issues began in 1870. These coins have always carried the portrait of the reigning British monarch on the obverse:

Victoria	1858–1901	George VI	1937–1952
Edward VII	1902–1910	Elizabeth II	1953 to date
George V	1911–1936		

Up to 1948, the monarch's title read *Rex et Ind: Imp* ("King and Emperor of India"). In Victoria's reign, the legend read *Regina et Ind: Imp* for "Queen and Empress of India." In 1948, *et Ind: Imp* was deleted because of the change in India's status.

In Canadian coinage, mint marks play a less important role than they do in United States coinage. Canadian coins have been struck at three different mints, but it has rarely happened that different mints have issued the identical denomination in the same year. Thus, Canadian coinage has practically none of those sensational variations in value that come about frequently when several mints turn out coins in the same year.

As far as mint marks are concerned, Canadian coins are classified as follows: H coins were struck at the Heaton Mint in Birmingham, England. Coins dated between 1858 and 1907, which bear no mint mark, were struck at the Royal Mint at London. Coins dated after 1907, with the C mint mark or no mint mark, were struck at the Royal Canadian Mint at Ottawa.

Two years of Canadian coinage were struck with special marks after the regular coinage for those years had already been completed. In 1937, a tiny dot was punched on the 1936 dies for the cent, 10-cent piece, and 25-cent piece. The resulting "dot" coinage resulted in the outstanding Canadian rarities as far as the cents and 10-cent coins were concerned.

In 1948, some coins were struck from the 1947 dies, with a tiny maple leaf added after the date to indicate that 1948 was the year of issue. In the tables, the notation "ML" indicates this.

For many years, the reverses of Canadian coins were quite plain, being limited to values and wreaths. But the first dollar, issued in 1935, was a radical departure. The first coinage of George VI in 1937 extended the change to all the other denominations. The colorful reverses that have appeared since that time place modern Canadian coins among the most picturesque and attractive coins ever issued.

The five-cent piece has gone through a number of transformations. Its silver content was dropped in 1922 in favor of nickel. During World War II, nickel was needed so badly that the coin was struck in tombac brass, an alloy of 88 percent copper and 12 percent zinc. As this alloy is easily confused with bronze, the new coin was given a twelve-sided shape.

In 1943, the tombac was retained, but the beaver on the reverse gave way to a torch and a "V" for victory. This design was continued in 1944 and 1945, but chromium-finished steel replaced tombac. In 1946, nickel was again used and the beaver reappeared. However, the new coins were still twelve sided.

From 1973 to 1976, Canada issued a long series of coins to commemorate and help finance the 1976 International Olympic Summer Games staged at Montreal. The series consisted of 28 sterling silver coins in $5 and $10 denominations and two gold pieces in $100 denominations.

Since 1977, Canada has issued on an annual basis $100 gold commemorative coins in proof condition. In October 1985, the Royal Canadian Mint began striking a series of ten $20 silver coins to publicize and help raise funds for the 1988 International Olympic Winter Games scheduled for Calgary, Alberta. In 1990, Canada began issuing $200 gold commemorative coins on an annual basis.

The 1994 $200 "Anne of Green Gables" coin pays tribute to the famous character in the novel by Canadian writer Lucy Maud Montgomery.

CANADIAN LARGE CENTS

PROVINCE OF CANADA

QUANTITY	YEAR	VERY GOOD	FINE	VERY FINE	UNC.
421,000	1858	$25.00	$30.00	$60.00	$200.00
9,579,000	1859	1.25	2.00	5.00	35.00
	1859 re-engraved date	20.00	25.00	50.00	125.00
	1859 over 58, wide 9	25.00	30.00	60.00	150.00
	1859 over 58, narrow 9	30.00	45.00	60.00	200.00

DOMINION OF CANADA

Mint marks on 1876, 1881, 1882, 1890, and 1907 issues are under date on reverse. Mint marks on 1898 and 1900 issues are above bottom rim on reverse.

QUEEN VICTORIA

QUANTITY	YEAR	VERY GOOD	FINE	VERY FINE	UNC.
4,000,000	1876 H	1.25	2.25	5.00	45.00
2,000,000	1881 H	1.75	3.00	10.00	55.00
4,000,000	1882 H	1.25	2.00	3.00	35.00
2,500,000	1884	1.50	2.25	5.00	40.00
1,500,000	1886	3.00	3.50	6.00	65.00
1,500,000	1887	2.50	3.00	5.50	50.00
4,000,000	1888	1.25	2.00	2.50	35.00
1,000,000	1890 H	4.00	7.00	10.00	125.00
1,452,537	1891 large date	4.00	6.00	10.00	80.00
	1891 small date, small leaves	30.00	40.00	65.00	325.00

QUANTITY	YEAR	VERY GOOD	FINE	VERY FINE	UNC.
	1891 small date, large leaves	40.00	50.00	85.00	350.00
1,200,000	1892	2.50	4.00	8.00	45.00
2,000,000	1893	1.75	2.75	4.00	30.00
1,000,000	1894	6.00	8.00	10.00	85.00
1,200,000	1895	3.00	5.00	6.00	45.00
2,000,000	1896	1.50	2.00	2.75	30.00
1,500,000	1897	1.50	2.00	2.75	35.00
1,000,000	1898 H	3.50	5.00	7.50	75.00
2,400,000	1899	1.25	2.00	3.00	35.00
1,000,000	1900	5.50	7.50	10.00	80.00
2,600,000	1900 H	1.50	2.50	3.50	37.50
4,100,000	1901	1.00	1.50	2.25	30.00

KING EDWARD VII

QUANTITY	YEAR	VERY GOOD	FINE	VERY FINE	UNC.
3,000,000	1902	1.10	1.50	2.75	20.00
4,000,000	1903	1.25	1.75	2.50	20.00
2,500,000	1904	1.50	2.50	3.50	32.50
2,000,000	1905	3.00	4.50	6.50	45.00
4,100,000	1906	1.25	2.00	3.00	20.00
2,400,000	1907	1.75	2.75	4.00	32.00
800,000	1907 H	7.50	11.00	20.00	125.00
2,401,506	1908	2.25	3.25	4.50	35.00
3,973,329	1909	1.25	1.75	2.50	25.00
5,146,487	1910	1.00	1.50	2.00	20.00

KING GEORGE V

QUANTITY	YEAR	VERY GOOD	FINE	VERY FINE	UNC.
4,663,486	1911	1.25	2.00	3.50	32.50
5,107,642	1912	.75	1.00	1.75	20.00
5,735,405	1913	.75	1.00	1.75	20.00
3,405,958	1914	1.25	1.75	2.50	37.50
4,932,134	1915	.85	1.35	2.25	20.00
11,022,367	1916	.50	1.00	1.50	17.50
11,899,254	1917	.50	1.00	1.25	15.00
12,970,798	1918	.50	.85	1.25	15.00
11,279,634	1919	.50	.85	1.25	15.00
6,762,247	1920	.50	1.00	1.35	17.50

CANADIAN SMALL CENTS

QUANTITY	YEAR	VERY GOOD	FINE	VERY FINE	UNC.
15,483,923	1920	.25	.40	1.50	15.00
7,601,627	1921	.25	.65	1.25	20.00
1,243,635	1922	7.50	10.00	20.00	135.00
1,019,002	1923	12.00	15.00	30.00	225.00
1,593,195	1924	3.00	5.50	8.50	100.00
1,000,622	1925	9.50	12.50	25.00	225.00
2,143,372	1926	2.00	3.50	5.00	85.00
3,553,928	1927	1.00	1.50	3.00	35.00
9,144,860	1928	.20	.35	.80	12.50
12,159,840	1929	.20	.35	.75	12.50
2,538,613	1930	1.50	2.00	3.50	37.50
3,842,776	1931	1.00	1.25	3.50	35.00
21,316,199	1932	.15	.25	.45	12.50
12,079,310	1933	.15	.25	.50	12.50
7,042,358	1934	.20	.30	1.00	15.00
7,526,400	1935	.15	.25	1.00	12.50
8,768,769	1936	.15	.25	1.00	12.50
678,823	1936 dot (outstanding rarity; only 5 known)				

KING GEORGE VI

QUANTITY	YEAR	VERY GOOD	FINE		
10,040,231	1937	.75	3.50		
18,365,608	1938	.50	3.50		
21,600,319	1939	.40	3.00		
85,740,532	1940	.25	2.00		
56,336,011	1941	.25	10.00		
76,113,708	1942	.30	12.50		
89,111,969	1943	.30	6.50		
44,131,216	1944	.25	5.00		
77,268,591	1945	.20	2.50		

CANADIAN SMALL CENTS (continued)

QUANTITY	YEAR	VERY GOOD	FINE
56,662,071	1946	.20	2.00
31,093,901	1947	.20	2.00
43,855,488	1947 ML	.20	2.50
25,767,779	1948	.50	2.75
32,190,102	1949	.15	1.75
60,444,992	1950	.15	1.50
80,430,379	1951	.15	1.25
67,633,553	1952	.15	.75

QUEEN ELIZABETH II

QUANTITY	YEAR	MS-65	QUANTITY	YEAR	MS-65
72,293,723	1953	1.00	329,695,772	1968	.20
21,898,646	1954	7.50	335,240,929	1969	.20
56,686,307	1955	1.00	311,145,010	1970	.10
78,685,535	1956	1.00	298,228,936	1971	.10
100,422,054	1957	.50	451,304,591	1972	.10
57,827,413	1958	.50	457,059,852	1973	.10
83,615,343	1959	.30	692,058,489	1974	.10
75,772,775	1960	.30	642,318,000	1975	.10
139,598,404	1961	.30	701,122,890	1976	.05
227,244,069	1962	.30	453,762,670	1977	.05
279,076,334	1963	.25	911,170,647	1978	.05
484,655,322	1964	.15	754,394,064	1979	.05
304,441,082	1965	.15	911,800,000	1980	.05
183,644,388	1966	.15	1,219,465,254	1981	.05
345,140,645	1967 dove reverse	.15	876,029,450	1982	.05

Beginning in 1982, the shape of the Canadian cent was changed from a round to a 12-sided coin in order to make it easier for the blind to identify.

QUANTITY	YEAR	MS-65	QUANTITY	YEAR	MS-65
997,820,210	1983	.05	696,629,000	1991	.05
838,235,000	1984	.05	—	1992	.05
782,752,500	1985	.05		1993	.05
740,335,000	1986	.05		1994	.05
918,549,000	1987	.05		1995	.05
482,676,752	1988	.05			
1,066,628,200	1989	.05			
205,377,000	1990	.05			

CANADIAN 5 CENTS SILVER
PROVINCE OF CANADA

QUANTITY	YEAR	VERY GOOD	FINE	VERY FINE	UNC.
1,500,000	1858 small date	$9.00	$15.00	$30.00	$250.00
	1858 large date	125.00	200.00	350.00	1100.00

DOMINION OF CANADA

The mint marks are below center of ribbon tying wreath on reverse.

QUEEN VICTORIA

QUANTITY	YEAR	VERY GOOD	FINE	VERY FINE	UNC.
2,800,000	1870	10.00	15.00	35.00	225.00
1,400,000	1871	7.50	14.00	30.00	250.00
2,000,000	1872 H	6.50	9.00	25.00	235.00
800,000	1874 H	8.00	12.50	35.00	350.00
1,000,000	1875 H	35.00	85.00	300.00	1500.00
3,000,000	1880 H	4.00	7.00	20.00	175.00
1,500,000	1881 H	4.50	8.00	20.00	200.00
1,000,000	1882 H	5.00	9.00	30.00	225.00
600,000	1883 H	10.00	16.00	50.00	350.00
200,000	1884	85.00	100.00	200.00	2000.00
1,000,000	1885	7.00	10.00	35.00	350.00
1,700,000	1886	4.00	8.00	20.00	275.00
500,000	1887	10.00	17.50	45.00	325.00
1,000,000	1888	4.00	6.50	15.00	175.00
1,200,000	1889	15.00	30.00	60.00	500.00
1,000,000	1890 H	4.50	7.00	20.00	200.00
1,800,000	1891	3.00	5.50	9.00	140.00
860,000	1892	5.00	10.00	15.00	200.00
1,700,000	1893	3.00	5.50	9.00	140.00
500,000	1894	10.00	15.00	37.50	275.00
1,500,000	1896	4.00	5.50	15.00	250.00
1,319,283	1897	4.00	5.50	15.00	200.00
580,717	1898	8.00	14.00	25.00	225.00
3,000,000	1899	2.50	4.00	7.00	130.00
1,800,000	1900 oval O	2.50	4.50	7.00	130.00
	1900 round O	14.00	35.00	50.00	350.00
2,000,000	1901	2.50	4.00	10.00	125.00

KING EDWARD VII

QUANTITY	YEAR	VERY GOOD	FINE	VERY FINE	UNC.
2,120,000	1902	1.50	2.50	3.00	65.00
2,200,000	1902 H (small H)	7.50	10.00	20.00	175.00
	1902 H (large H)	2.00	2.50	5.00	65.00
1,000,000	1903	4.00	6.50	20.00	200.00
2,640,000	1903 H	2.50	4.00	10.00	125.00
2,400,000	1904	2.50	4.00	10.00	150.00
2,600,000	1905	2.50	4.00	10.00	125.00
3,100,000	1906	2.00	3.00	7.50	100.00
5,200,000	1907	1.75	3.00	7.50	100.00
1,220,524	1908	7.50	10.00	17.50	125.00
1,983,725	1909	2.50	3.50	10.00	150.00
5,850,325	1910	1.50	2.50	3.00	80.00

KING GEORGE V

QUANTITY	YEAR	VERY GOOD	FINE	VERY FINE	UNC.
3,692,350	1911	2.50	4.00	10.00	125.00
5,863,170	1912	1.50	2.50	5.00	65.00
5,588,048	1913	1.50	2.50	5.00	50.00
4,202,179	1914	1.50	2.50	5.00	65.00
1,172,258	1915	10.00	12.50	25.00	325.00
2,481,675	1916	2.50	3.00	5.00	100.00
5,521,373	1917	1.25	2.00	3.50	65.00
6,052,298	1918	1.25	2.00	3.50	50.00
7,835,400	1919	1.25	2.00	3.00	50.00
10,649,851	1920	1.50	2.25	4.00	50.00
2,582,495	1921 rare—only about 50 known				
		1500.00	2000.00	3000.00	16,500.00

Note: Choice BU specimen, finest known, sold at Stack's Dec. 1989 sale for $57,200.

CANADIAN 5 CENTS NICKEL

KING GEORGE V

QUANTITY	YEAR	VERY GOOD	FINE	VERY FINE	UNC.
4,794,119	1922	$.40	$1.00	$3.50	$65.00
2,502,279	1923	.65	1.50	5.00	100.00
3,105,839	1924	.50	1.00	4.50	90.00
201,921	1925	30.00	40.00	90.00	800.00
938,162	1926 Near 6	3.00	4.50	30.00	350.00
	1926 Far 6	80.00	125.00	200.00	1500.00

CANADIAN 5 CENTS NICKEL (continued)

QUANTITY	YEAR	VERY GOOD	FINE	VERY FINE	UNC.
5,285,627	1927		1.00	3.50	60.00
4,577,712	1928		1.00	3.50	60.00
5,611,911	1929		1.00	3.50	60.00
3,704,673	1930		1.00	3.50	80.00
5,100,830	1931		.75	3.00	80.00
3,198,566	1932		.75	3.00	100.00
2,597,867	1933		1.00	3.50	125.00
3,827,304	1934		.75	3.00	100.00
3,900,000	1935		.75	3.00	100.00
4,400,450	1936		.75	3.00	65.00

KING GEORGE VI

QUANTITY	YEAR	VERY FINE	UNC.
4,593,263	1937	2.50	27.50
3,898,974	1938	3.25	95.00
5,661,123	1939	1.75	55.00
13,920,197	1940	1.25	30.00
8,681,785	1941	1.00	37.50
6,847,544	1942	1.00	32.50
3,396,234	1942 tombac	1.50	5.00
24,760,256	1943 tombac	.75	4.00
11,532,784	1944 chrome steel	.50	3.50
18,893,216	1945 chrome steel	.40	3.50
6,952,684	1946	.60	9.00
7,603,724	1947	.60	9.00
9,595,124	1947 ML	.60	9.00
1,810,789	1948	2.50	25.00
12,750,002	1949	.40	6.00
4,970,520	1950	.40	6.00
8,329,321	1951 nickel commemorative	.25	3.50
4,313,410	1951 steel	.35	7.00
10,892,877	1952 steel	.25	5.00

QUEEN ELIZABETH II

QUANTITY	YEAR	VERY FINE	MS-65
16,638,218	1953 steel	.25	5.00
6,998,662	1954 steel	.25	10.00
5,356,020	1955 nickel	.15	4.00
9,399,854	1956 nickel		3.50
7,329,862	1957 nickel		3.50
7,592,000	1958 nickel		1.50
11,552,523	1959 nickel		.85
37,157,433	1960		.50
47,889,051	1961		.35
46,307,305	1962		.25
43,970,320	1963		.25
78,075,068	1964		.25
84,876,019	1965		.20
27,678,469	1966		.50
58,884,849	1967 rabbit reverse		.25
99,253,330	1968		.25
27,830,229	1969		.15
5,726,010	1970		.15
27,312,609	1971		.15
62,417,387	1972		.15
53,507,435	1973		.15
94,704,645	1974		.15
138,882,000	1975		.10
55,140,213	1976		.10
89,120,791	1977		.10
137,079,273	1978		.10
186,295,825	1979		.10
134,878,000	1980		.10
99,104,272	1981		.10
105,532,450	1982 copper nickel		.10
33,220,210	1983 copper nickel		.10
84,088,000	1984 copper nickel		.10

114 CATALOG OF CANADIAN COINS

QUANTITY	YEAR	MS-65
126,168,000	1985 copper nickel	.10
148,158,000	1986 copper nickel	.10
106,299,000	1987 copper nickel	.10
75,025,000	1988 copper nickel	.10
141,435,538	1989 copper nickel	.10
42,402,000	1990 copper nickel	.10

QUANTITY	YEAR	MS-65
46,693,000	1991 copper nickel	.10
	1992 copper nickel	.10
	1993 copper nickel	.10
	1994 copper nickel	.10
	1995 copper nickel	.10

CANADIAN 10 CENTS SILVER

The mint marks are below center on ribbon tying wreath on reverse.

QUEEN VICTORIA

QUANTITY	YEAR				
1,250,000	1858	$11.00	$17.50	$45.00	$325.00
1,600,000	1870	8.00	14.00	35.00	350.00
800,000	1871	11.00	20.00	50.00	400.00
1,870,000	1871 H	16.50	25.00	55.00	500.00
1,000,000	1872 H	55.00	100.00	200.00	750.00
600,000	1874 H	7.00	12.50	30.00	350.00
1,000,000	1875 H	150.00	225.00	500.00	3500.00
1,500,000	1880 H	5.50	12.50	20.00	300.00
950,000	1881 H	7.50	17.50	35.00	375.00
1,000,000	1882 H	6.00	12.50	30.00	350.00
300,000	1883 H	17.50	35.00	125.00	1000.00
150,000	1884	100.00	250.00	425.00	4500.00
400,000	1885	17.50	25.00	100.00	1200.00
800,000	1886	12.00	25.00	65.00	425.00
350,000	1887	20.00	40.00	125.00	1500.00
500,000	1888	5.00	9.00	30.00	375.00
600,000	1889	350.00	550.00	1200.00	8000.00
450,000	1890 H	10.00	20.00	50.00	475.00
800,000	1891	9.00	20.00	40.00	400.00
520,000	1892	8.50	15.00	30.00	350.00
500,000	1893 round top				
		3400.00	700.00	1300.00	8750.00
	1893 flat top	312.00	25.00	65.00	475.00
500,000	1894	6.50	11.00	50.00	400.00
650,000	1896	6.50	11.00	25.00	325.00
720,000	1898	6.50	11.00	25.00	325.00
1,200,000	1899	4.00	7.00	20.00	275.00
1,100,000	1900	3.00	6.25	25.00	225.00
1,200,000	1901	3.00	6.25	25.00	225.00

KING EDWARD VII

QUANTITY	YEAR				
720,000	1902	4.00	7.00	20.00	250.00
1,100,000	1902 H	3.00	5.00	12.50	150.00
500,000	1903	7.00	12.50	60.00	800.00
1,320,000	1903 H	3.00	5.00	20.00	300.00
1,000,000	1904	7.00	12.50	35.00	325.00
1,000,000	1905	5.00	10.00	35.00	325.00
1,700,000	1906	4.00	7.00	25.00	250.00
2,620,000	1907	3.00	5.00	15.00	215.00
776,666	1908	4.00	11.00	25.00	350.00
1,697,200	1909 with				
	1908 leaves	5.00	10.00	35.00	325.00
	1909 broad				
	leaves	6.00	12.00	40.00	400.00
4,468,331	1910	2.50	5.50	12.50	175.00

KING GEORGE V

QUANTITY	YEAR				
2,737,584	1911	10.50	15.00	30.00	225.00
3,235,557	1912	1.50	2.50	10.00	200.00
3,613,937	1913 broad				
	leaves	90.00	150.00	300.00	4250.00
	1913 (1914				
	leaves)	1.25	2.50	12.50	200.00
2,549,811	1914	1.50	3.00	10.00	175.00
688,057	1915	6.50	12.50	35.00	650.00

10 CENTS SILVER: KING GEORGE V (continued)

QUANTITY	YEAR	VERY GOOD	FINE	VERY FINE	UNC.
4,218,114	1916	1.00	1.50	5.00	150.00
5,011,988	1917	1.00	1.50	3.50	100.00
5,133,602	1918	1.00	1.50	3.50	100.00
7,877,722	1919	1.00	1.50	3.50	100.00
6,305,345	1920	1.00	1.50	4.00	100.00
2,469,562	1921	1.25	2.00	4.00	125.00
2,458,602	1928	1.25	1.75	4.50	100.00
3,253,888	1929	1.25	1.75	4.50	100.00
1,831,043	1930	1.50	3.00	5.50	100.00
2,067,421	1931	1.50	2.75	6.00	100.00
1,154,317	1932	1.75	3.00	7.50	125.00
672,368	1933	2.00	5.00	8.50	135.00
409,067	1934	3.50	5.00	9.00	225.00
384,056	1935	3.50	7.50	20.00	375.00
2,460,871	1936	1.50	2.00	4.00	90.00
192,194	1936 dot (4 known)				37,500.00

KING GEORGE VI

QUANTITY	YEAR	VERY GOOD	FINE	VERY FINE	UNC.
2,499,138	1937	2.50	3.50	5.25	27.50
4,197,323	1938	1.50	2.75	5.00	70.00
5,501,748	1939	1.50	2.00	8.00	50.00
16,526,470	1940	1.50	1.75	3.50	25.00
8,716,386	1941	1.50	1.75	4.50	75.00
10,214,011	1942	1.50	1.75	3.00	50.00
21,143,229	1943	1.50	1.75	3.00	20.00
9,383,582	1944	1.50	1.75	3.00	32.50
10,979,570	1945	1.50	1.75	2.00	20.00
6,300,066	1946		1.75	2.00	35.00
4,431,926	1947		1.75	3.50	50.00
9,638,793	1947 ML		1.75	2.00	20.00
422,741	1948	4.50	8.00	12.50	90.00
11,120,006	1949			2.00	10.00
17,823,595	1950			2.00	10.00
15,079,265	1951			2.00	10.00
10,476,340	1952			2.00	7.50

QUEEN ELIZABETH II

QUANTITY	YEAR	VERY FINE	MS-65
18,467,020	1953	1.50	7.50
4,435,795	1954	2.50	15.00
12,294,649	1955	1.50	6.00
16,732,844	1956	1.75	12.50
15,631,952	1957		2.00
10,908,306	1958		3.00
19,691,433	1959		1.50
45,446,835	1960		1.50
26,850,859	1961		1.50
41,864,335	1962		1.50
41,916,208	1963		1.50
49,518,549	1964		1.50
56,965,392	1965		1.50
34,330,199	1966		1.50
63,012,417	1967 mackerel reverse		1.50
70,460,000	1968 .500 fine silver		1.00
172,582,930	1968 pure nickel		.75
55,833,929	1969		.65
5,249,296	1970		.50
41,016,968	1971		.35
60,169,387	1972		.35
167,715,435	1973		.35
201,566,565	1974		.35
207,680,000	1975		.35
95,018,533	1976		.20
128,452,206	1977		.20

QUANTITY	YEAR	UNC.	QUANTITY	YEAR	UNC.
170,366,431	1978	.20	162,998,558	1988	.20
236,910,479	1979	.20	198,695,414	1989	.20
169,742,000	1980	.20	64,400,000	1990	.20
123,899,272	1981	.20	46,693,000	1991	.20
93,953,450	1982	.20		1992	.20
111,920,210	1983	.20		1993	.20
119,080,000	1984	.20		1994	.20
143,025,000	1985	.20		1995	.20
156,400,000	1986	.20			
147,309,000	1987	.20			

CANADIAN 20 CENTS SILVER

750,000	1858	$60.00	$85.00	$125.00	$1250.00

CANADIAN 25 CENTS SILVER

The mint marks are below center of ribbon tying wreath on reverse.

QUEEN VICTORIA

900,000	1870	12.00	20.00	60.00	650.00
400,000	1871	12.00	20.00	70.00	950.00
748,000	1871 H	15.00	25.00	85.00	850.00
2,240,000	1872 H	6.50	11.00	30.00	500.00
1,600,000	1874 H	6.50	11.00	30.00	500.00
1,000,000	1875 H	175.00	450.00	1000.00	6500.00
400,000	1880 H narrow "O"	20.00	50.00	125.00	1000.00
	1880 H wide "O"	70.00	125.00	350.00	2500.00
820,000	1881 H	10.00	20.00	60.00	650.00
600,000	1882 H	14.00	25.00	80.00	750.00
960,000	1883 H	8.50	14.00	60.00	650.00
192,000	1885	70.00	130.00	300.00	3000.00
540,000	1886	10.00	20.00	75.00	1000.00
100,000	1887	55.00	100.00	250.00	2750.00
400,000	1888	10.00	20.00	60.00	650.00
66,324	1889	65.00	110.00	400.00	4000.00
200,000	1890 H	15.00	27.50	80.00	1100.00
120,000	1891	35.00	65.00	185.00	1400.00
510,000	1892	8.50	18.00	50.00	650.00
100,000	1893	45.00	90.00	300.00	1750.00
220,000	1894	12.50	25.00	80.00	900.00
415,580	1899	5.00	9.00	30.00	475.00
1,320,000	1900	5.00	7.50	20.00	350.00
640,000	1901	5.00	7.50	17.50	350.00

KING EDWARD VII

464,000	1902	6.00	10.00	35.00	500.00
800,000	1902 H	5.00	7.50	20.00	325.00
846,150	1903	5.00	12.00	35.00	450.00
400,000	1904	10.00	25.00	80.00	900.00

25 CENTS SILVER: KING EDWARD VII (continued)

QUANTITY	YEAR	VERY GOOD	FINE	VERY FINE	UNC.
800,000	1905	6.00	12.00	40.00	700.00
1,237,843	1906	5.00	12.00	35.00	450.00
2,088,000	1907	5.00	10.00	25.00	375.00
495,016	1908	6.50	12.00	50.00	500.00
1,335,929	1909	5.00	8.00	25.00	450.00
3,577,569	1910	4.00	9.00	20.00	300.00
KING GEORGE V					
1,721,341	1911	15.00	28.00	70.00	550.00
2,544,199	1912	3.50	6.50	15.00	300.00
2,213,595	1913	3.50	6.50	15.00	275.00
1,215,397	1914	3.50	6.00	15.00	350.00
242,382	1915	10.00	22.50	100.00	2500.00
1,462,566	1916	3.25	5.00	15.00	250.00
3,365,644	1917	3.25	4.50	12.50	150.00
4,175,649	1918	3.25	4.50	12.50	130.00
5,852,262	1919	3.25	4.50	12.50	130.00
1,975,278	1920	3.50	5.00	16.00	150.00
597,337	1921	9.00	20.00	80.00	1250.00
468,096	1927	20.00	40.00	100.00	1500.00
2,114,178	1928	3.25	4.50	11.00	200.00
2,690,562	1929	3.25	4.50	11.00	200.00
968,748	1930	4.00	5.50	12.50	300.00
537,815	1931	3.75	6.50	18.00	375.00
537,994	1932	4.00	7.00	18.00	350.00
421,282	1933	4.00	7.50	20.00	325.00
384,350	1934	4.00	7.50	20.00	400.00
537,772	1935	4.00	6.50	15.00	325.00
972,094	1936	3.25	6.00	12.50	150.00
153,685	1936 dot	30.00	65.00	175.00	1750.00
KING GEORGE VI					
2,689,813	1937	3.25	5.25	12.50	30.00
3,149,245	1938	3.25	5.25	12.50	100.00
3,532,495	1939	3.25	5.25	12.50	90.00
9,583,650	1940	3.25	5.25	9.00	27.50
6,654,672	1941	3.25	5.25	9.00	27.50
6,935,871	1942	3.25	5.25	9.00	27.50
13,559,575	1943		4.75	7.00	27.50
7,216,237	1944		4.75	7.00	35.00
5,296,495	1945		4.75	7.00	30.00
2,210,810	1946		4.75	7.00	55.00
1,524,554	1947		4.75	8.00	500.00
4,393,938	1947 ML		5.25	8.00	25.00
2,564,424	1948			9.00	65.00
7,864,002	1949			6.00	17.50
9,673,335	1950			6.00	15.00
8,285,599	1951			6.00	15.00
8,861,657	1952			6.00	15.00

QUEEN ELIZABETH II

QUANTITY	YEAR	MS-65
11,141,851	1953	$10.00
2,318,891	1954	50.00
9,552,505	1955	12.50
11,269,353	1956	8.00
12,364,001	1957	4.50
9,743,033	1958	4.50
13,503,461	1959	3.50
22,835,327	1960	3.25
18,164,368	1961	3.25
29,559,266	1962	3.25
21,180,652	1963	3.25
36,479,343	1964	3.25
44,708,869	1965	3.00
25,388,892	1966	3.00
48,863,764	1967 wildcat reverse	3.00
71,500,000	1968 .500 silver	3.00

QUANTITY	YEAR	MS-65
88,686,931	1968 pure nickel	1.00
133,037,929	1969	1.00
10,300,000	1970	1.00
48,100,000	1971	1.00
43,743,387	1972	1.00

QUANTITY	YEAR	MS-65	QUANTITY	YEAR	MS-65
134,958,587	1973 RCMP Comm.	1.00	158,734,000	1985	.50
192,360,598	1974	.85	119,280,000	1986	.50
141,148,000	1975	.85	53,408,000	1987	.50
86,898,261	1976	.50	80,368,475	1988	.50
99,634,555	1977	.50	119,624,307	1989	.50
176,475,408	1978	.50	31,140,000	1990	.50
131,042,905	1979	.50	459,000	1991	.50
76,178,000	1980	.50		1992	.50
131,580,272	1981	.50		1993	.50
167,414,450	1982	.50		1994	.50
13,920,210	1983	.50		1995	.50
119,212,000	1984	.50			

CANADIAN 50 CENTS SILVER

The mint marks are below center of ribbon tying wreath on reverse.

QUEEN VICTORIA

QUANTITY	YEAR	VERY GOOD	FINE	VERY FINE	UNC.
450,000	1870	$200.00	$750.00	$1000.00	$12,500.00
200,000	1871	50.00	120.00	300.00	4000.00
45,000	1871 H	80.00	165.00	375.00	4500.00
80,000	1872 H	37.50	70.00	250.00	4500.00
150,000	1881 H	35.00	60.00	200.00	4000.00
60,000	1888	90.00	185.00	500.00	6500.00
20,000	1890 H	550.00	1000.00	2250.00	18,500.00
151,000	1892	40.00	80.00	200.00	5000.00
29,036	1894	165.00	300.00	1000.00	12,000.00
100,000	1898	40.00	80.00	300.00	5000.00
50,000	1899	80.00	160.00	425.00	8000.00
118,000	1900	35.00	70.00	175.00	3500.00
80,000	1901	40.00	80.00	215.00	3500.00

KING EDWARD VII

QUANTITY	YEAR	VERY GOOD	FINE	VERY FINE	UNC.
120,000	1902	20.00	50.00	135.00	1500.00
140,000	1903 H	30.00	65.00	200.00	2000.00
60,000	1904	85.00	175.00	425.00	5000.00
40,000	1905	100.00	200.00	500.00	6500.00
350,000	1906	17.50	37.50	100.00	1600.00
300,000	1907	17.50	37.50	100.00	1500.00
128,119	1908	25.00	60.00	180.00	1500.00
203,118	1909	17.50	50.00	125.00	1500.00
649,521	1910	12.50	30.00	100.00	1350.00

KING GEORGE V

QUANTITY	YEAR	VERY GOOD	FINE	VERY FINE	UNC.
209,972	1911	17.50	85.00	350.00	2000.00
285,867	1912	10.00	18.50	70.00	1750.00
265,889	1913	10.00	18.50	70.00	1750.00
160,128	1914	22.50	65.00	185.00	2850.00
459,070	1916	10.00	17.50	55.00	900.00
752,213	1917	8.50	15.00	30.00	750.00
854,989	1918	8.50	15.00	30.00	625.00
1,113,429	1919	8.50	15.00	30.00	700.00
584,691	1920	8.50	15.00	30.00	850.00
206,398	1921*	8000.00	10,000.00	14,000.00	37,500.00
228,328	1929	8.50	15.00	37.50	800.00
57,581	1931	12.50	22.50	70.00	1500.00
19,213	1932	50.00	80.00	225.00	2000.00
39,539	1934	17.50	32.50	85.00	1500.00
38,550	1936	17.50	32.50	70.00	1000.00

*Note: Outstanding rarity. Choice MS-65 specimen sold at Bowers-Merena Sept. 1989 sale for $110,000.

KING GEORGE VI

QUANTITY	YEAR	VERY GOOD	FINE	VERY FINE	UNC.
192,016	1937		10.00	12.50	60.00
192,018	1938		12.00	20.00	265.00
287,976	1939		10.00	12.50	160.00
1,996,566	1940		9.00	10.00	35.00
1,974,165	1941		9.00	10.00	35.00
1,974,165	1942		9.00	10.00	35.00
3,109,583	1943		9.00	10.00	32.50

50 CENTS SILVER: KING GEORGE VI (continued)

QUANTITY	YEAR	FINE	VERY FINE	UNC.
2,460,205	1944	$9.00	$10.00	$32.50
1,959,528	1945	9.00	10.00	32.50
950,235	194	9.00	10.00	80.00
424,885	1947			
	straight 7	10.00	12.50	135.00
	1947			
	curved 7	9.00	12.00	125.00
38,433	1947 ML			
	straight 7	35.00	50.00	200.00
	1947 ML			
	curved 7	100.00	1500.00	3500.00
37,784	1948	60.00	100.00	250.00
858,002	1949	9.00	12.00	50.00
2,384,179	1950	8.50	10.00	30.00
2,421,010	1951	8.50	10.00	17.50
2,598,337	1952	8.50	10.00	17.50

QUEEN ELIZABETH II

QUANTITY	YEAR	MS-65
1,781,191	1953	20.00
506,305	1954	50.00
753,511	1955	25.00
1,379,499	1956	15.00
2,171,689	1957	10.00
2,957,200	1958	10.00
3,095,535	1959	10.00
3,488,897	1960	8.50
3,584,417	1961	8.50
5,208,030	1962	8.50
8,348,871	1963	8.50
9,377,676	1964	8.50
12,629,974	1965	8.50
7,683,228	1966	8.50
4,221,135	1967 wolf reverse	10.00
3,966,932	1968 pure nickel	

QUANTITY	YEAR	MS-65
.	(smaller planchet)	1.25
7,113,929	1969	1.25
2,429,526	1970	1.25
2,166,444	1971	1.25
2,515,632	1972	1.25
2,546,096	1973	1.25
3,436,650	1974	1.25
3,710,000	1975	1.25
2,940,719	1976	1.00
709,839	1977	5.50
3,341,892	1978	1.00
3,425,000	1979	1.00
1,574,000	1980	1.00
2,692,272	1981	1.00
2,877,124	1982	1.00
1,920,210	1983	1.00
1,502,989	1984	1.00
2,188,374	1985	1.00
779,400	1986	1.00
373,000	1987	1.00
220,000	1988	1.00
266,419	1989	1.00
207,000	1990	1.00
490,000	1991	1.00
	1992	1.00
	1993	1.00
	1994	1.00
	1995	1.00

CANADIAN SILVER DOLLARS
KING GEORGE V

QUANTITY	YEAR	FINE	VERY FINE	UNC.
428,707	1935	$20.00	$25.00	$75.00
306,100	1936	17.50	22.50	70.00
	KING GEORGE VI			
241,002	1937	17.50	25.00	60.00
90,304	1938	28.50	35.00	135.00

QUANTITY	YEAR	FINE	VERY FINE	UNC.
1,363,816	1939 Parliament buildings	11.00	12.50	28.50
38,391	1945	150.00	200.00	350.00
93,055	1946	30.00	40.00	150.00
65,595	1947 blunt 7	50.00	75.00	165.00
	1947 pointed 7	100.00	175.00	500.00
21,135	1947 ML	125.00	200.00	475.00
18,780	1948	375.00	600.00	1000.00
641,840	1949 ship (Newfoundland commem.)	17.50	25.00	45.00
261,002	1950	12.50	14.00	37.50
411,395	1951	12.00	13.50	22.50
408,835	1952	12.00	13.50	22.50

QUEEN ELIZABETH II

QUANTITY	YEAR		VERY FINE	MS-65
1,087,265	1953		12.50	17.50
242,815	1954		13.50	27.50
274,810	1955		13.50	27.50
209,092	1956		15.00	35.00
496,389	1957		12.50	17.50
3,390,564	1958 Totem Pole (British Columbia Commem.)		20.00	
1,443,502	1959			12.50
1,420,486	1960			12.50
1,262,231	1961			12.50
1,884,789	1962			12.50
4,179,981	1963			12.50
7,296,832	1964			12.50
10,768,569	1965			12.50
9,912,178	1966			12.50

QUANTITY	YEAR	UNC.
6,694,571	1967 goose reverse	20.00
5,579,714	1968 pure nickel (smaller planchet)	3.50
4,809,313	1969	3.50
4,140,058	1970 (Manitoba Centennial)	4.00
4,260,781	1971 (British Columbia Centennial) nickel	4.00
555,564	1971 (British Columbia Centennial) silver	20.00
2,676,041	1972 nickel	4.00
350,109	1972 Voyageurs silver	20.00
3,196,452	1973 (Prince Edward Island Centennial) nickel	4.00
904,795	1973 (Royal Canadian Mounted Police Centennial) silver	17.50
2,799,363	1974 (Winnipeg Centennial) nickel	4.00
628,183	1974 (Winnipeg Centennial) silver	17.50
833,095	1975 (Calgary Centennial) silver	17.50

CANADIAN SILVER DOLLARS (continued)

QUANTITY	YEAR	UNC.	PROOF-65
2,498,204	1976 Voyageurs nickel	4.00	
483,722	1976 (Parliament Library) silver	22.50	
1,393,745	1977 Voyageurs nickel	17.50	
847,194	1977 (Elizabeth II Silver Jubilee) silver	17.50	
744,655	1978 (XI Commonwealth Games) silver	17.50	
2,954,842	1979 Voyageurs nickel	5.00	
913,818	1979 (The *Griffon*) silver	15.00	

QUANTITY	YEAR	MS-65	
3,291,221	1980 Voyageurs nickel	3.00	
552,439	1980 (Arctic Territories) silver	17.50	
2,775,272	1981 Voyageurs nickel	3.00	
699,494	1981 (Railroad) silver	15.00	
3,391,624	1982 Voyageurs nickel	2.50	
903,888	1982 (Regina Centennial) silver	15.00	
11,812,000	1982 (Constitution Centennial) nickel	2.50	
2,720,210	1983 Voyageurs nickel	2.50	
159,450	1983 (World University Games, Edmonton) silver	12.50	
340,068	1983 (World University Games, Edmonton)		17.50
7,009,323	1984 (Jacques Cartier 400th anniversary of the voyage to Canada) nickel	2.50	
87,760	1984 (Jacques Cartier 400th anniversary of the voyage to Canada)		10.00
133,610	1984 (Toronto Sesquicentennial) silver	12.50	
570,940	1984 (Toronto Sesquicentennial)		17.50
162,873	1985 (National Parks, Moose) silver	12.50	
727,247	1985 (National Parks, Moose)		17.50
124,574	1986 (Centennial of Vancouver) silver	12.50	
672,642	1986 (Centennial of Vancouver)		17.50
117,147	1987 (Davis Straits) silver	12.50	
587,102	1987 (Davis Straits)		17.50
199,300,000	1987 (Common Loon) nickel		2.00
178,120	1987 (Common Loon)		20.00
106,702	1988 (St. Maurice ironworks) silver	12.50	
259,230	1988 (St. Maurice ironworks)		17.50
138,893,539	1988 (Common Loon) nickel	2.00	
	1988 (Common Loon)		12.50
110,650	1989 (Bicentennial of Mackenzie River discovery) silver	12.50	
272,319	1989 (Bicentennial of Mackenzie River discovery)		17.50
184,773,902	1989 (Common Loon) nickel	2.00	
	1989 (Common Loon)		12.50
99,206	* 1990 (300th anniversary of exploration of the Canadian prairies by Henry Kelsey) silver	12.50	

*The obverse of Canada's Henry Kelsey 1990 commemorative silver dollar bears a new effigy of Queen Elizabeth II by Dora dePedery Hunt (replacing the previous design by Arnold Machin used from 1965 to 1989). This is the first time an effigy of Elizabeth II by a Canadian artist has appeared on coinage.

QUANTITY	YEAR	UNC.	PROOF-65
254,634	1990 (300th anniversary of the exploration of the Canadian prairies by Henry Kelsey)		17.50
68,402,000	1990 (Common Loon) nickel	2.00	
140,649	1990 (Common Loon)		12.50
73,843	1991 ("S.S. Frontenac") silver	15.00	
195,824	1991 ("S.S. Frontenac")		22.50
23,156,000	1991 (Common Loon) nickel	2.00	
	1991 (Common Loon)		20.00
	1992 (Stagecoach Service) silver	15.00	
	1992 (Stagecoach Service)		22.50
	1992 (Common Loon) nickel	2.00	
	1992 (Common Loon)		22.50
	1992 (Parliament, 125th Anniversary of Confederation) nickel	2.00	

QUANTITY	YEAR	UNC.	PROOF-65
	1992 (Parliament, 125th Anniversary of Confederation)		22.50
	1993 (Common Loon) nickel	2.00	
	1993 (Common Loon)		22.50
	1993 (Stanley Cup Hockey Centennial)	17.50	
	1993 (Stanley Cup Hockey Centennial)		25.00
	1994 (Common Loon) nickel	2.00	
	1994 (Common Loon)		22.50
	1994 (Royal Canadian Mounted Police Dog Team Patrol)	17.50	25.00
	1994 (National War Memorial) bronze/nickel	15.00	20.00
	1995 (Common Loon) nickel	2.00	
	1995 (Common Loon)		22.50
	1995 (325th Anniversary of the Hudson's Bay Company in Canada)	17.50	25.00
	1995 (Peacekeeping, 50th Anniversary of the United Nations)	15.00	20.00

CANADIAN SILVER 5 DOLLARS
QUEEN ELIZABETH II

Series I	UNC.	PROOF
1973 (Olympic Games Commemorative—sailboats)	$20.00	
1973 (Map of North America)	20.00	

Series II		
1974 (Olympic Games Commemorative—Olympic Rings)	$20.00	$35.00
1974 (Athlete with torch)	20.00	35.00

Series III		
1974 (Rowing)	20.00	35.00
1974 (Canoeing)	20.00	35.00

Series IV		
1975 (Marathon)	20.00	35.00
1975 (Ladies' javelin throwing)	20.00	35.00

Series V		
1976 (Swimmer)	20.00	35.00
1976 (Diver)	20.00	35.00

Series VI		
1976 (Fencing)	20.00	35.00
1976 (Boxing)	20.00	35.00

Series VII		
1976 (Olympic Village)	20.00	35.00
1976 (Olympic flame)	20.00	35.00

CANADIAN SILVER 10 DOLLARS

Series I		
1973 (Olympic Games Commemorative— Montreal skyline)	35.00	50.00
1973 (Map of World)	35.00	50.00

Series II		
1974 (Head of Zeus)	35.00	50.00
1974 (Temple of Zeus)	35.00	50.00

Series III		
1974 (Cycling)	35.00	50.00
1974 (Lacrosse)	35.00	50.00

Series IV		
1975 (Men's hurdles)	35.00	50.00
1975 (Ladies' shot put)	35.00	50.00

Series V		
1975 (Sailing)	35.00	50.00
1975 (Paddler)	35.00	50.00

Series VI		
1976 (Football) $35.00	$50.00	
1976 (Field Hockey)	35.00	50.00

Series VII		
1976 (Olympic Stadium)	35.00	50.00
1976 (Olympic Velodrome)	35.00	50.00

OLYMPIC $100 GOLD COINS

QUANTITY	YEAR	PROOF
650,000	1976 (.583 gold)	$150.00
350,000	1976 (.917 gold, reduced size)	200.00

COMMEMORATIVE $100 GOLD COINS

QUANTITY	YEAR	PROOF
180,396	1977 (Elizabeth II Silver Jubilee)	275.00
200,000	1978 (Canadian Unification)	250.00
250,000	1979 (Year of the Child)	250.00
300,000	1980 (Arctic Territories)	250.00
102,000	1981 (National Anthem)	250.00
122,000	1982 (New Constitution)	250.00
83,000	1983 (St. John's Newfoundland, 400th Anniversary)	275.00
200,000	1984 (Jacques Cartier, 400th anniversary of voyage to Canada)	250.00
200,000	1985 (National Parks)	250.00
200,000	1986 (International Year of Peace)	250.00
145,175	1987 (1988 Summer Olympics Torch and Rings)	250.00
52,239	1988 (Bowhead Whale)	250.00
63,881	1989 (350th Anniversary of Ste. Marie Among the Hurons—the first European Settlement in Ontario)	250.00
49,518	1990 *(International Literacy Year)	250.00
33,966	1991 (S.S. *Empress of India*)	250.00
	1992 (Montreal 350th Anniversary)	250.00
	1993 (The Horseless Carriage)	250.00
	1994 (Home Front World War II)	250.00
	1995 (275th Anniversary of the Founding of Louisbourg)	250.00

CANADIAN GOLD SOVEREIGNS

QUANTITY	YEAR	VERY FINE	UNC.
636	1908 C	1850.00	3750.00
16,273	1909 C	300.00	900.00
28,012	1910 C	260.00	700.00
	KING GEORGE V		
3,715	1913 C	600.00	1250.00
14,891	1914 C	325.00	850.00
6,111*	1916 C	20,000.00	32,500.00
58,845	1917 C	130.00	225.00
106,516	1918 C	130.00	225.00
135,889	1919 C	130.00	225.00

The mint marks are above the date on the reverse.

* Rare, about 20 known. Choice BU specimen, finest known, sold for $82,500 at Stack's Dec. 1989 sale.

5 DOLLARS GOLD
KING GEORGE V

165,680	1912	200.00	400.00
98,832	1913	200.00	400.00
31,122	1914	500.00	950.00

10 DOLLARS GOLD
KING GEORGE V

74,759	1912	450.00	900.00
149,232	1913	450.00	900.00
140,068	1914	550.00	1200.00

20 Dollars Gold

20 DOLLARS GOLD
QUEEN ELIZABETH II

337,512	1967 (proof only)	250.00

1988 WINTER OLYMPIC GAMES, CALGARY

$20 Silver Set of Ten

QUANTITY	ITEM	EVENT	RELEASE DATE	PROOF
359,522	(1)	Downhill Skiing	Oct. 1985	$40.00
311,830	(2)	Speed Skating	Oct. 1985	40.00
345,203	(3)	Ice Hockey	March 1986	40.00
280,188	(4)	Biathlon	March 1986	40.00
267,790	(5)	Cross-Country Skiing	Sept. 1986	40.00
263,820	(6)	Free-Style Skiing	Sept. 1986	40.00
283,720	(7)	Figure Skating	March 1987	40.00
253,220	(8)	Curling	March 1987	40.00
246,651	(9)	Ski-Jumping	Sept. 1987	40.00
216,709	(10)	Bobsledding	Sept. 1987	40.00

Gold Bullion Trade ("Maple Leaf")

Since 1979, Canada has annually issued a gold bullion trade coin containing exactly one troy ounce of gold. Called the "Maple Leaf" it has a nominal denomination of $50. Beginning in 1982, fractional Maple Leafs were minted: a $5 denomination containing $1/10$ troy ounce of gold and a $10 denomination containing $1/4$ troy ounce of pure bullion.

On July 29, 1993, during the American Numismatic Association Convention at Baltimore, the Royal Canadian Mint unveiled two new members of its Maple Leaf bullion coin investment program: the $1/20$ ounce gold and platinum coins. Both are denominated at $1.

Then on Sept. 9, 1994, the Royal Canadian Mint inaugurated two new values in its bullion coin investment family: the $1/15$ ounce gold and platinum coins. Both are denominated at $2.

1987 Canadian $50 "Maple Leaf" Gold Bullion Coin

Platinum Bullion and Collectors Coins

Since 1988 Canada has annually issued a series of platinum bullion trade coins which are nominally denominated at $5, $10, $20, and $50 and contain $\frac{1}{10}$, $\frac{1}{4}$, $\frac{1}{2}$ and 1 troy ounce of pure bullion, respectively. Prices vary according to bullion quotations, which in early-to-mid-1995 fluctuated between $405/450 per ounce.

Starting in 1990, the Royal Canadian Mint has been producing sets of four platinum coins designed especially for collectors. These carry nominal denominations of $30, $75, $150, and $300 and contain $\frac{1}{10}$, $\frac{1}{4}$, $\frac{1}{2}$ and 1 troy ounce of pure bullion, respectively.

The 1990 set depicts polar bears, while the 1991 set portrays the snowy owls native to Canada. All platinum coins bear the obverse portrait of Elizabeth II. The 1992 set portrays Cougars, the 1993 set depicts Arctic Foxes, and the 1994 set features Sea Otter.

Mintage for each coin has been limited to 3,500.

Silver Bullion Coins

Since 1988 Canada has annually issued a silver bullion coin nominally denominated at $5. The coin, containing exactly one troy ounce of silver, portrays Elizabeth II on obverse and the Canadian Maple leaf on reverse.

Canadian Confederation 125th Anniversary Issue

In 1992 Canada issued a set of 13 coins commemorating the 125th anniversary of Confederation. Reverse designs for all 13 coins in the "Canada 125" coin program were chosen in an open competition. Obverse of each coin has the Elizabeth II portrait.

Throughout 1992 the Royal Canadian Mint issued one quarter dollar coin in silver from January through December, one for each of the country's 12 provinces and territories. In July, RCM issued a "Confederation Dollar" in nickel-plated silver in proof. Though legal tender, the coins are not intended to circulate. Mintage for each coin was set at 10 million.

25 CENTS SILVER

ITEM	NAME	RELEASE DATE	BU PROOF
(1)	New Brunswick	Jan. 1992	$10.00
(2)	Northwest Territories	Feb. 1992	10.00
(3)	Newfoundland	March 1992	10.00
(4)	Manitoba	April 1992	10.00
(5)	Yukon	May 1992	10.00
(6)	Alberta	June 1992	10.00
(7)	Prince Edward Island	July 1992	10.00
(8)	Ontario	August 1992	10.00
(9)	Nova Scotia	Sept. 1992	10.00
(10)	Quebec	Oct. 1992	10.00
(11)	Saskatchewan	Nov. 1992	10.00
(12)	British Columbia	Dec. 1992	10.00

THE SILVER DOLLAR

Canadian Confederation	July 1992	20.00

COMMEMORATIVE $100 GOLD COINS

QUANTITY	YEAR	PROOF
33,966	1991 Sailing ship "Empress of India"	
	1992 (350th anniversary of the founding of Montreal)	

SILVER DOLLARS

QUANTITY	YEAR	MS-65	PROOF-65
23,156,000	1991 (Common Loon) nickel	2.00	
	1991 (Common Loon)		12.50
73,843	1991 *Frontenac* (175th anniversary of the sailing ship)		17.50
195,424	1991 *Frontenac*	25.00	
	1992 (Common Loon) nickel	2.00	
	1992 (Common Loon)		12.50
	1992 (175th anniversary of stagecoach service between Kingston and Toronto)	17.50	25.00

$20 SILVER/GOLD*

QUANTITY	YEAR	PROOF
29,162	1990 (Powered Flight in Carada/The First 50 Years, "Anson" "Harvard," Pilot Robert Leckie)	$50.00
28,997	1990 (Powered Flight in Canada/The First 50 Years, "Lancaster," Pilot John Fauquier)	50.00
28,791	1991 (Powered Flight in Canada/The First 50 Years, "A.E.A. Silver Dart," Designer John A.D. McCurdy and Pilot Casey Baldwin)	50.00
29,399	1991 (Powered Flight in Canada/The First 50 Years, The "de Havilland Canada Beaver," Pilot Phillip C. Garratt)	50.00
56,000	1992 (Powered Flight in Canada/The First 50 Years)	50.00
50,000	1992 (Powered Flight in Canada/The First 50 Years)	50.00
	1993 ("Fairchild 71C," Powered Flight in Canada/The First 50 Years)	50.00
	1993 ("Lockheed 14 Super Electra," Powered Flight in Canada/The First 50 Years)	50.00
	1994 ("Curtiss HS-2L," Powered Flight in Canada/The First 50 Years)	50.00
	1994 (Canadian "Vickers Vedette," Powered Flight in Canada/The First 50 Years)	50.00

* The Powered Flight in Canada Coins are unusual because the cameo portraits are .999 gold and are superimposed over .999 sterling silver.

COMMEMORATIVE $200 GOLD COINS

QUANTITY	YEAR	PROOF
18,040	1990 Canadian flag carried aloft, Honors the Spirit and Promise of Canada's Youth	$375.00
8,741	1991 ("Hockey—a National Passion" Celebrates Canada's Youth)	375.00

COMMEMORATIVE $200 GOLD COINS (continued)

QUANTITY	YEAR	PROOF
	1992 (Niagara Falls)	375.00
25,000	1993 (Royal Canadian Mounted Police)	375.00
	1994 (Anne of Green Gables)	375.00

1992 Olympic Centennial Set

Canada has joined forces with four other countries (Australia, France, Austria and Greece) to commemorate the centennial of the modern Olympic Games, with the five nations agreeing to strike three coins each, one in gold and two in silver.

The modern Olympic games were started in Athens in 1896, and thus all 15 coins carry the "1896–1996" dates underneath the interlocking-rings Olympic emblem.

Canada took the honor of commencing the five-nation series of coins in 1992 and is to be followed by Australia, France, Austria and Greece from 1993–96.

The Canadian gold coin (containing approximately a ½ troy ounce of bullion) is nominally denominated at $175, while the two silver coins (containing a troy ounce of bullion each) are denominated at $15.

All 15 coins are inscribed with the Latin motto "Citius Altius Fortius" (faster, higher, stronger).

Silver   Gold

QUANTITY	YEAR	PROOF-65
	1992 Speed Skater, Pole Vaulter and Gymnast $15 Silver	
	1992 "Spirit of the Generations of Athletes" $15 Silver	400.00
35,000	1992 The Olympic Flame $175 Gold	

The Royal Canadian mint for the first time in its history will begin striking $2 coins for circulation in 1996. It is expected that this coin will be struck in nickel/bronze.